A CHRISTIAN ANTHROPOLOGY

Religious Experience Series

Edward J. Malatesta, S.J., General Editor

Volumes in Preparation:

Religious Experience Series

Volume 2

A Christian Anthropology

by

Joseph Goetz, S.J., Bernard Rey, Edouard Pousset, S.J.,
André Derville, S.J., Aimé Solignac, S.J.,
Robert Javelet, Albert Ampe

Translated by
Sister Mary Innocentia Richards, S.N.J.M.

With a Preface by
Robert Faricy, S.J.

ABBEY PRESS
St. Meinrad, Indiana 47577
1974

The present work is a translation of the articles "Homme" and "Homme intérieur" which first appeared in the *Dictionnaire de Spiritualité,* Paris, Beauchesne, 1969, vol. 7, cols. 617-650 and 650-674 respectively.

Preface

by Robert Faricy, S.J.

This book is concerned with what has come to be called "Christian anthropology." The word "anthropology" is understood here not in its usual scientific sense, as applying to a specific science, but in a more general way as a reflection on man, his nature, his meaning, his purpose. In this broad sense, anthropology is a *logos* about *anthropos,* a word about man, the study of who and what man is.

Christian anthropology, then, is the study of man in a Christian perspective. It is a reflection on man as he is, but a reflection that takes place within a properly Christian framework. It is the study of man in the light of Christ. And this means that it is theological.

What is theology as it is understood today, and what place in theology has Christian anthropology? In the first place, theology is distinguished from the scientific disciplines of religious studies. These scientific disciplines include, for example, the sociology of religion, religious psychology, the history of religion, and the comparative study of religions. They include also biblical exegesis, the study of the formation of the Old and New Testaments, and Church history. These areas are scientific in the modern sense of the word "science." They call for objectivity, for a certain distance from what is being studied. They are concerned with particulars, with objective descriptions and analyses of religious behavior, or with historical facts, or with the meaning of biblical words or phrases in a particular historical and cultural context.

The term "theology" is today increasingly reserved to those disciplines that are concerned not with particulars but with the totality of God's revelation in Christ. These disciplines study the whole of Christian revelation, each from its own special point of view. This includes all doctrinal theology, for example, dogmatic theology, spiritual theology, pastoral theology, moral theology, liturgical theology. Theology is concerned with the whole kerygma, with the complete good news in Christ. It tries to bring into formulation, always in new ways for new times, God's word. Theology brings God's word to expression.

Since the totality of Christian revelation is contained in the person of the risen Christ, God's word is, ultimately, God's Word, the person of Jesus. Theology, because it is not concerned with particulars but with a totality, and because it is centered not on a set of data but on a person, is not really a science. It is true that theology is a "science" in the medieval sense of the word, a *scientia,* a special intellectual discipline that has its own methods, data, principles, perspectives, and unity. But it is not a science in the usual sense that the word "science" has today.

Theology is, as has been repeated for centuries, "faith seeking understanding." It operates out of a faith commitment. The truth about which theology is concerned is not a truth that can be divided up into separate parts; unlike science, theology studies—not particulars—but a totality, the whole "good news" of God's revelation to man in Jesus Christ. Furthermore, the truth that theology tries to bring to expression is, at the most profound level, the person of Jesus Christ. It is, therefore, a truth that is not only to be understood, but a truth that is to be responded to. So, again unlike science, theology contains a strong subjective element, for it works out of the subjective matrix of a personal faith commitment.

In the past twenty-five years or so, theologians have come to a deeper understanding of the faith dimension of theology. Besides this, there is today, especially in Catholic theology, general agreement on the subject matter of theology, on what theology studies. Theology studies man and his world in the light of Christ. This is, of course, not to say that theology does not concern God; but it talks about God in terms of God's relationship with man and man's world, a relationship that is centered in Jesus Christ. Theology is, then, in a broad sense, Christian understanding of man, Christian anthropology. What this means in practice is that any theology—and there are as many theologies as there are theologians—depends on the theologian's conception of man. That is to say, a theology depends on how the theologian sees man, and the world around man, in relation to God; but this depends finally on that theologian's understanding of man, his nature, activities, and purpose.

This can be put in a different way. Any Christian theology depends on two sources: God's revelation in Christ as understood in a particular Christian tradition, such as Catholicism; and, secondly, some generally philosophical framework within which that revelation is formulated and organized. Karl Rahner, for example, views Christian revelation in terms of his own brand of Thomism, heavily influenced by the philosophies of Joseph Maréchal and the modern German phenomenologists and existentialists. Again, Pierre Teilhard de Chardin's theology is a result of interpreting certain elements of Christian revelation, as found especially in the writings of St. Paul and St. John, within the perspective of Teilhard's own theory of evolution and social progress.

Any theologian, then, works with two sources, with two sets of data: Christian revelation, and some general philosophical matrix in terms of which the data of revelation can be understood. This second set of data, this philosophical framework, is always centered on some particular understanding of man. Thus, the differences between theologies depend to a great extent on different ideas of man. For theology is Christian anthropology, and so how man is understood is the chief determining element of any theology.

We can distinguish here two senses of the phrase "Christian anthropology." The first sense is a broad one; in this sense, all Christian theology is Christian anthropology. In a second and narrower sense, Christian anthropology can be understood as the study of man as such in the light of Christ. In this second and stricter sense, Christian anthropology is the foundation stone of any theology, and the base upon which are constructed, for example, theological understandings of the Church, the sacraments, moral conduct, and the spiritual life.

What is the importance of the theological study of man, of Christian anthropology in the strict sense, for spirituality? Progress in union with God depends, for the most part, on growth in the understanding of self in relation to Christ. Personal relationship with Christ is at the center of Christian living. This is not to diminish the importance of community, or of service, or of personal reflection and study. It is to say that all of these are important, but that what they depend on is a personal relationship with God. This central relationship with God, in which God relates the Christian to Himself in Christ, is the axis of Christian growth and the organizing and integrating relationship of all of the Christian's other relationships—to other persons, to his work, to the world around him. And growth in personal relationship with Jesus Christ depends on growth in the Christian's understanding of himself as this particular person who is known completely and personally by Christ, accepted totally and even chosen by Him, loved not impersonally, but by name, personally.

This growth in Christian self-understanding is chiefly a product of prayer. For relationship with Jesus Christ is an interpersonal relationship, and so its mainspring is interpersonal communication, a conscious being-with, sharing, responding; and this is what prayer is. Nevertheless, theological understanding can promote Christian growth by contributing to prayer, by being a base and background for prayer. This is the relationship between theological study and prayer. Theology is ordered to better Christian life, and the center of Christian life is prayer. In this sense, theology is ordered to prayer, is for prayer.

Theological reflection on man can help the individual Christian to deepen his own understanding of himself as a Christian. By better understanding man (in general) in the light of Christ, he can, hopefully, better understand himself in relation to Christ.

It is the theological study of man, Christian anthropology in the strict sense, that is the focus of this book. Even more exactly, the book is designed to be a work instrument, a study tool, in the area of the study of man (as such) in the light of Christ. Each of the various authors considers man from a special point of view.

The first chapter, on man as understood in primitive cultures, is not theological, but rather pretheological, a sort of prologue to the other chapters. It is of interest especially as a background (or, better, foreground) to the biblical idea of man. The author, Joseph Goetz, is a well known French cultural anthropologist. In this first chapter, he uses his long experience in the area of anthropology, both in field work and in teaching, to generalize the pertinent conclusions of the contemporary science of anthropology.

The second chapter, "Man in Christ," is a study of the relationship which, in Christ, is established between the believer and God, as this relationship is expressed in the writings of St. Paul. A commentary on God's plan for man in the first two chapters of Genesis leads up to a description of man with God in Christ as found in St. Paul's letters. This chapter is, then, a study of "man" in St. Paul, and a Pauline theology of man.

Chapter three, "Christian Man in Dialectic," is a theological reflection on the data of Scripture as interpreted in Christian tradition, a reflection within the framework of the neo-Hegelian philosophy of the Rev. Gaston Fessard, S.J., written by a former student of his, and long-time friend, Father Edouard Pousset, S.J. Since Fessard's theology of man is essentially Pauline as well as dialectical in the Hegelian sense, this chapter serves as a theological development of the preceding chapter. Father Pousset's presentation of Fessard's theology is a model of concision and clarity; and it is a great boon to English-speaking readers, among whom Fessard's thought is not nearly as well known as it is in Europe.

The four chapters on "interior man" treat a specific aspect of Christian existence, personal interiority, from the point of view of the historical development of the idea of the interior man. An appreciation of the development of interior man in the history of Christian thought is fundamental to a contemporary Christian understanding of man. This is because, up until the modern era, the Christian notion of what man is, of how he is made in his reason and his will, of how he is specifically different from the animals and intrinsically in some kind of special relationship with God—this whole complex notion of what man is in the light of Christ has evolved to a great extent within the framework of the concept of interior man.

It is hoped that the material published here, translated from the French of the *Dictionnaire de Spiritualité,* will be helpful in deepening theological understanding and stimulating theological reflection, and that it will lead the reader to a better theological understanding of man as a partial basis for a better understanding of himself in his relationship with Jesus Christ.

Robert L. Faricy, S.J.
Rome

List of Abbreviations

ACW	Ancient Christian Writers	Westminster, Md.
CF	Cistercian Fathers	Washington, D.C.
DS	*Dictionnaire de Spiritualité*	Paris
FC	Fathers of the Church	New York; Washington, D.C.
NPNF	Nicene and Post-Nicene Fathers	Grand Rapids (reprint)
RAM	*Revue d'ascétique et de mystique*	Toulouse
SC	*Sources chrétiennes*	Paris
TDNT	Theological Dictionary of the New Testament	Grand Rapids

Contents

Part One

Man

Introduction

Writing on "man" today is an undertaking that presents many difficulties and pitfalls. For one thing there is the temptation to try to cover too much ground. There is no question here of presenting an exhaustive collection of monographs on the many approaches to the study of man such as the history of religions, cultural anthropology, sociology, psychoanalysis, history, and others. Nor is there any attempt here to describe the study of man in the history of Christian thought; such an endeavor would have to include serious consideration not only of biblical anthropology but also of the stoicism and platonism of the Fathers of the Church as well as the great medieval syntheses. There is a further difficulty. At a time when behavioral sciences are emphasizing man's conditioning, is it possible to continue to speak of philosophical anthropology?

These are some of the problems that were confronted in the planning of this study and that justify the choices adopted.

The work has three parts. The short study on primitive man is included as a brief exploration into the area of human sciences. The study of man in Christ is less an essay on biblical anthropology than it is a presentation of Christian existence, of the relationship which, in Christ, may be established between the believer and God. The reflections of a philosopher on man neither aim at going beyond contemporary questions nor at giving explicit answers to them. Rather, they aim to "outline a way" by showing the basic categories of human life and by comparing them with Christian life.

Chapter I

Man in Primitive Religions

by Joseph Goetz, S.J.

A study of the understanding of man held by primitive peoples may well be compared with studies of the Old Testament view of man and of the idea of man in the thought of the Greek philosophers before Plato.

In all three of these cases, understandings are with difficulty translated into value systems and categories of our traditional philosophy. There is more than a difference of concepts; there is a different manner, existential and experiential, of looking at man in his being and in his activities.

A. *The Human Being*

Among primitive peoples, the words *body* and *soul* do not have the meaning we give to them, or to be more exact, they have no equivalent. The celebrated reply of the Melanesians of New Caledonia to M. Leenhardt is well known. He asked them what the white people brought them; "the body," said they. When cultural anthropologists speak of peoples who recognize in man as many as twelve souls, it is impossible to take this word *soul* in its usual meaning.

In trying to summarize this difficult phenomenology, we must note first of all that the body is neither a prison from which the soul is waiting to be freed, nor is it that co-principle from which the soul is separated at death, while waiting, after a period of existence in a violent or abnormal situation, until it

3

will once again be reunited to its body. Life with a body is a
moment or a transitory experience of the ego. The body is an
instrument, an organ, made use of by the ego in one of the
stages of existence. The life of the ego is not bound to it,
even before death; rather, the body is one of the ego's numerous "appurtenances" spoken of by Lévy-Bruhl. During sleep,
in dreams, and in certain magic activities, the self can travel
and act far from its living body. All that the "body" will undergo during that time will affect its distant double, and all that
this traveling "soul" will experience will react and have an effect
on its "body." Even after death the destruction of the body or
deprivation of burial will touch the soul in its very life. The
body is only one of the numerous aspects or "accessories" of
the self. In the same way the numerous souls are only manifestations or aspects of the self, and for the same reason as the
body, distinct but interdependent. At the moment of death the
breath leaves; then the self loses one of its manifestations
which is reintegrated into the world while continuing to belong
to it in its new state. It is the same for the shade. One can
still distinguish the character (the Greek *thumos*) of the phantom, a manifestation of the self after death. Finally, the self
or a certain aspect of the self of an ancestor may, after his
death, be reincarnated in one of his descendants or in an animal, without ceasing, at the same time, to reside in the land of
the dead. The state of the dead man himself is a condition of
the ego, brought about by the rites which have as their purpose
the transformation of the dead man as a deceased person, that
is to say, to give him a new and exact status, more or less
definitive, in another life. There is something more. A living
person is able to lose his "soul," stolen or devoured by a
sorcerer, without on that account ceasing to live at least for a
certain time. Indeed, to assure his security, an individual can
place his soul in an object or in an animal; but if this object
or this animal is destroyed, he will soon die.

We cannot reason about the representations of the primitives by applying our concepts to them or by translating them
into our vocabulary. The body, before or after death, breath,
personal temperament, shade, conscience, intelligence, phantom,
the double, are aspects of the self which manifest it at determined moments of its existence and which are united one with

the other by a same principle, the ego, even when they are scattered in time and space. Therefore, the ego is capable of simultaneous and interdependent multi-presences, of which none contains it exclusively. These forms are "accessories," such as the name, the hair, the bones that make one think of it, but also allow acting upon it as they permit it to be present and acting. If we wish to speak of soul and body, it is the ego and the person that must be understood by that; and each one of the elements ought to be regarded as one of its modes of being. Each one of its manifestations, body or soul, is it, to the extent that the destruction of one of these elements is the destruction of the ego under that precise form, that is to say, the suppression of the possibility of manifesting the self under that form or at that level.

To understand such concepts, one must not search their source in reasoning or logical deductions. For example, we cannot say that the idea of survival after death has been suggested to primitive peoples by the demands of justice that would make them hope for another life where there would be compensation, under certain conditions, for the deficiencies of existence here below. In general, aside from the advantages involving the physiology of the body, the dead find in the other world the same state of existence as in this world. The rich will be rich; the lepers will be lepers (except when the incurable diseases are looked upon as something from God, for in that case they go into the house of God); slaves will be slaves. What is essential is to be in the group and there to take up again one's activity. There is the assurance of collective survival, which, doubtless, is nothing more than the feeling that what exists cannot cease to exist. Only those are excluded from this collective survival who in this life have injured the existence of the group, such as sorcerers, or those who have been abandoned by the group, such as the dead who have been deprived of burial. Basically, survival is an experience where, being present in thought, heritage, heredity, memory, is being present objectively; for to exist is to be perceived.

Another aspect of survival may help to understand these representations. Often a second death is spoken of. At the end of a certain time, the dead of whom no one thinks any longer, or whose memory fades away, generally after the fourth generation, melt into a sort of anonymous mass or into the cosmos. Here again we find the notion of manifestation that is essential to this type of anthropology. What is present to the consciousness of the living is regarded as being according to the manner in which it is perceived. Primitive peoples start out from a point of view different from us; and they hold to it. Essences and definitions do not interest them. Their whole thought is centered on existence, its manifestations, its conditions, and particularly on the involvements that the manifestations demand of us. We can only translate their concepts into an existential phenomenology.

B. *The Human Condition*

Man is not the center of the universe, and he is not the measure of things. Let us simply consider totemism. However, since it is man who considers his function, not as an individual but as a person, that is to say, as an individual essentially socialized, he sees his function as basic to the development of the cosmos. He is the weakest and most uncertain element in it, but he is conscious of its order and of his role and, therefore, feels himself responsible. It is true that primitive cosmogonies are crowned by the apparition of man and many of them are only anthropogonies. The civilizing hero or world creator has the function of making the world habitable for man. But in addition to the fact that this hero is himself a man, typical man, he may appear long after the first humanity. He is the organizer and prototype of human existence as we live it, we who see and think. Man's whole thought has no other objective than to discover how he is placed in this world and how he is to adjust himself to it, lest he compromise the order in which he is placed, and as a result compromise his very existence. What is more, at a stage of more complex existential thought, such as the Mexican cosmogonies, the concern of the gods in creating man is to find a being who will serve them and guarantee their well-being.

The thought of the primitives is taken up therefore with the view of knowing and understanding at each moment the cosmic circumstances in order to discover the role they are to play in them at that moment; this they must do in the light of the facts. In itself that which is does not interest them, except in the measure that it determines an attitude. Here arises the problem of the opposition between religion and magic.

Magic is knowledge or know-how that claims to subject the elements to man's will. It claims to know laws and techniques which would permit the ruling of all powers according to man's caprice. One of the most striking aspects of primitive societies is their horror of sorcery, which is nothing more than magic applied to the pursuit of individual ends considered as antisocial, social being understood as being in solidarity with the group and with the cosmos. On the other hand, magic is simply the application of a world concept respected with as much exactitude and humility as science. Man rules only by submitting himself with exactitude to the laws of the universe as he knows it. That is why the gods reveal and accept magic when they know man will practice it in an orderly fashion. Therefore, magic that does not deviate toward sorcery has a religious aspect, namely, submission to an order within which to reign is to serve. Magic and religion are often placed in opposition, magic being understood as having the idea of an active, impersonal world, while religion would see order in the world as an effect of a will that is personal and free. But magic and religion are not really incompatible any more than are science and religion. It is not necessary to think of order willed by God as static and nominalist.

The feeling of belonging to a whole is expressed at first by submission of the individual to society, to the group. It has been said and repeated since the time of Auguste Comte that among the primitives the individual does not exist as such, that he exists only as a member of a group. One is mistaken in concluding that the primitives lack personality. On the contrary, their present descendants see in personalism the truest expression of their feeling of existing. Indeed, for them, if the individual does not exist, it is because they see him only as a person, that is to say, an individual endowed with relationships and responsibilities in the collectivity and therefore endowed with a function. For them, the idea of rights and duties is replaced by the idea of function, a responsibility one does not choose but takes upon himself scrupulously because the existence of the whole is conditioned by it. This goes to the extent of the apparent nonexistence of a personal conscience, in the sense that an individual accused of disturbing by his existence or behavior the security of the whole group submits without question to its sanctions, even to death, although he has no consciousness of having done that of which he is accused. However, this is not completely exact, for there is a limit to this passivity. There is an appeal to the judgment of God in the depths of conscience, "God sees me," and this is the very moment when the judgment of the group is accepted.

The deep tendency of the primitive is to feel he exists only by and for the group. In defining this group-morality, one must add that the group as the primitive conceives it does not only include men, living or dead, or yet to be born, but also animals, vegetation, the elements, and the entire cosmos. It is very striking in clan-organization, which is so characteristic that some propose replacing the equivocal term *primitives* by that of *clan-peoples*. However, this term is too ambiguous by non-specialists as well as for cultural anthropologists. The clan-system is something very exact and brought about in diverse ways, the fundamental structure of which is common to almost all primitives. The human group is an ensemble of which each segment or subgroup has definite solidarities with seasonal rituals, with animal or vegetable aspects of the environment, with the dead, and with the landscape. Each individual is an organic member of the group, which is itself an organ of the All. The sum of these solidarities weaves a web that includes the known world. This universe is perceived as a great living body in which the behavior of each group and of each individual favors or compromises the existence of the totality. Ordinary actions become rituals, and these are the symbolic and real responses of the cosmogony in which are expressed the participation in the relationship of man to the All. Each attitude reproduces a universal model, and the ensemble of models constitutes the order of the universe. The terms *cosmic body* and *mystical body* come to mind spontaneously as soon as we wish to clarify this manner of seeing life and its relationships. Indeed, the parable of the members and the body is a very old theme not found solely among the ancient Romans.

It may be stated that the (dialectical) opposition of the

individual versus the group and of man versus the universe, although it exists basically and emerges as the idea of God, was not developed at the ethnological levels of human cultures. The primitives belong to a first moment that is orientated in an inverse direction to that of the individualism of the great cultures. The nature of beings is not thought about; the idea of man does not stand out clearly from the other categories of created things. The reason for this is not the incapacity to conceive a global or abstract view of the universe, but rather an orientation that is fundamentally existential. Man comes to a realization of himself because of his solicitude to assure his existence and his coexistence in the All. He is aware of all his experiences without reducing them to a theoretical system. For him the coherence stemming from the objective homogeneity of his experiences suffices. He even expresses this coherence in archetypes and myths that summarize his experiences. Above all he is imbued with the feeling that he is part of an interdependent whole that has laws and that imposes functions, just as he himself is an ensemble of diverse and interdependent manifestations. He even knows that beyond the All there is another center of reference on which all depends, but which comes into play only when man has exhausted every means of integration taught him by the experience found in tradition. He can enter into dialogue with God, because like Him he is immersed in the whole while exceeding its limits. His dignity lies in the exactitude and loyalty with which he fulfills his function as a member of the mystical body. He is a community-man, understanding "community" in the sense of going beyond a human society.

One of the most surprising facets of this organic concept of the universe is the place held by death in primitive societies. On the one hand, the king, being the central organ of the group, and therefore of the world, must be put to death and replaced by someone younger as soon as his vitality lessens, because this vitality is that of all the people. On the other hand, rituals for putting to death accompany all the stages and changes of the individual, of the group, or of their world. Being put to death, along with new and symbolic births of the young when they reach maturity, rites for chieftains, priests, and the shamans when they begin their functions, all of these call for initiation rituals. The symbolic or realistic putting to death of men, animals, and even plants at each change in nature from one cycle to another, at each crisis of society or of nature: these are celebrations of the mysteries of existence. This actualization of man's participation in that which constitutes the heart of biological existence, namely, the reciprocal liaison of death and new life applied to the entire cosmos, is not proper to agrarian societies which have expressed this in the parable of the seed. It is found very often and very dramatically in groups that have never known agriculture, especially in the composition and symbolism of prehistoric paintings. It is the expression and consecration of the central point of man's vision and of the world as an organic unit where man sees himself as a participating element collectively and, accordingly, individually responsible as a conscious member of the cosmic body. It is the empirical perception of a fact and the active adherence to a situation. Not knowing the profound meaning or the ontological structure of their world, primitive peoples are not concerned with making distinctions between God and other parts of reality. They simply take seriously the physical and spiritual interactions of all the elements of the world they live in.

Chapter 2

Man in Christ

by Bernard Rey

Preliminary Remarks

1. *Limits of the subject.* This chapter does not propose, strictly speaking, a sketch of a Christian anthropology, or even a description of what is sometimes called "biblical man." Encyclopedias and biblical dictionaries already propose such offerings, certain aspects of which are studied in the DS: flesh, heart, body, spirit. Furthermore, the DS has already devoted several articles to the great subjects of Christian life (Baptism, Charity, Church, Hope, Holy Spirit, Eucharist, Gospel, Faith.) There is no question of treating here, even in a synthetic way, the points developed in these studies.

Without ignoring these various aspects of Christian life, the present chapter will study their foundation, in order to know *the relationship which, in Christ, is established between the believer and God,* and which in a strict sense characterizes and constitutes the Christian man, the man of the New Covenant.

2. *Method and outline.* Since the beginning of Christianity, each age has had theologians and saints who tried to examine closely and to live this relationship between the believer and God. On this subject the thinking of the Fathers of the Church and the great spiritual writers would merit our attention. To keep this chapter within its correct proportions, we shall here limit ourselves to the offerings of the New Testament and

11

more particularly to the teachings of St. Paul. Moreover, this
choice is expressed in the title of the chapter, since the expression "in Christ" is the translation of the Pauline formula *(en
Christo)*. It is justified by the amplitude and content of the
epistles of the Apostle who was often led by the particular
situation of his ministry among the Gentiles to recall, in the
presence of Jews and pagans, the originality and radical newness of the Christian person: "Therefore, if any one is in
Christ, he is a new creation" (2 Cor 5:17; see Gal 6:15).[1]

This chapter will comprise three parts. First, God's plan
for man will be recalled, as we find it in the first chapter of
Genesis, the thought of which deeply inspired the Pauline
theology. The second part will make clear how Christ, in His
person, fulfilled God's plan. Then we will be able to show
in a more detailed way how it is by his union with Christ that
the Christian realizes his vocation as man.

A. *Man's Vocation according to Genesis 1-2*

1. According to the *Yahwist account* (Gn 2), man, in other
words the human race *(âdâm)*, is placed in the center of creation, and the image of the potter, used by the author, expresses all God's solicitude in man's regard (Gn 2:7). All
has been created for him. In the form of the garden of Eden,
the earth is confided to his keeping (2:15), the animals are
subject to him since man gives them their names, signifying
they are his (2:20). Man alone is not confided to the dominion of man, and the relationships between man and wife are
established on equality and love (2:18-25). The relationship
of man to the rest of earthly creation, of which God constitutes
him the master, does not exhaust (is not the measure of)
man's vocation. His condition in this world is established
basically on his situation in the sight of God. Drawn from the
earth, man is flesh, weak, and by himself he can but go back
to the earth (Gn 6:3). If he lives, it is because God has endowed him with the life that makes him a living being: "then
the Lord God formed man of dust from the ground, and
breathed into his nostrils the breath of life; and man became a
living being" (2:7). Man's existence is dependent on the spirit
of life that comes from God; it depends likewise on his obedience to the Word of Him who created it. If he does not ob-

serve the command of his Creator, he will die (2-17); that is to say, the life that made him to be will return to God, its source, while man will go back to the earth from which he was drawn (Gn 3:19); see Jb 10:9-12; Wis 15:7-11).

2. More recent, the *priestly account* (Gn 1) takes up the main points of the preceding narrative and states them more theologically, perhaps reacting, according to certain exegetes, to the anthropomorphisms of the Jahwist author. The privileged love of God for man, man's dominion over creation, his dependence on his Creator, themes of the first account, are found again and crystallize around the idea of God's image.

"Then God said, 'Let us make man in our image, after our likeness; and let them have dominion over the fish of the sea, and over the birds of the air, and over the cattle, and over all the earth, and over every creeping thing that creeps upon the earth.' So God created *(bara')* man in His own image, in the image of God He created him; male and female He created them. And God blessed them, and God said to them, 'Be fruitful and multiply, and fill the earth and subdue it; and have dominion over the fish of the sea and over the birds of the air and over every living thing that moves upon the earth' (1:26-28).

In this account, God's attention in the creation of man is no longer explained by the action of the potter (Gn 2:7). It is suggested by repeating the verb *bara'* (and perhaps also by the plural "Let us make ... to our image," a reflective plural, tending to bring out the idea of the care used by the Creator in the making of his masterpiece). We know that the Bible reserves exclusively to God the verb *bara';* only He is the subject of it. Originally, this word means "to show something new," something "unprecedented," that which is proper to God. We note that in the priestly account this solemn verb is used five times. By its use in Gn 1:1, resumed in inclusive form in Gn 2:4a, the author presents the whole of the work of six days as a prodigy of God. In Gn 1:21, in relation to the making of the "great sea serpents," he intends to cut short the old cosmogonic accounts that portrayed creation as a struggle of the gods with already existing monsters. In Gn 1:27, where it appears twice, the mention of this verb intends, therefore, to draw the reader's attention to the beauty and special importance of man's creation.

Indeed, man enjoys a special dignity among all creatures because he resembles God. Anyone who will shed man's blood will impair God's image (Gn 9:6). The words translated by "image" and "resemblance" correspond respectively to the Hebrew *celem* and *demût*. The first means an exterior representation and implies a physical similarity. The second implies a more general resemblance. Therefore, it explicates that if man is created in the image of God, there is no question of a substantial identity. Created in the image of God, man is not God: he is His creature and depends on Him. Care must be taken not to see in this resemblance a similarity in the physical order. The conclusions of philology must be delicately shaded because the Hebrew mentality was not accustomed, as we are, to distinguish between body and spirit, exterior and interior. This "resemblance" means that man is like God and is the only one among earth's creatures, a person to whom God speaks and who answers Him (see Gn 1:28-30; 2:7). Accordingly, man is the most beautiful of earth's creatures because he is God's partner and bears the divine likeness which sin will not be able to efface (Gn 9:6), and which he will transmit to his descendants (5:1-3).

This dignity also stands out because of the mission God entrusts to man. It will be noted to what a degree Gn 1:26-28 (text quoted above) closely links in man the fact of his being the image of God with his dominion over all things (see also Ps 8:4-7). Thus, man is set apart. On earth he is the Creator's delegate, the one who represents Him. God is the master of all things on earth and in heaven, but He entrusts to man the dominion of earth's creatures, asking him to subjugate all. By giving life, man will imitate God who gives life to all things; and he will fill the earth. By subjugating all, he will imitate God, the Lord of heaven and earth.

3. *Summary and conclusion.* According to the accounts in Genesis, the vocation of man, the image of God, is to represent God in the world. This task has a dual aspect. By their mutual love man and woman give life and "fill the earth." Man will have to exercise dominion over the world and subjugate it because all has been created for him. This dual task by which man "imitates" God, the source of life and ruler of

the universe, is indissolubly linked in the Bible with man's position before his Creator. It is as a creature that he peoples the earth and subdues it. This indicates that he accomplishes his mission in the service of God, to whom, ultimately, he must submit and to whom he must restore all things. Man is created free, but he must remain dependent on Him who gives him life. If he can subdue all things, he himself must submit to his Creator and obey His word. By creation, God in His love makes a covenant with man, makes him His friend, His co-worker. God remains God, and this covenant is bound up with the homage man gives his Creator and with his obedience to the sovereign will of the master of all things.

We know how Adam, the ancestor and figure of man according to the biblical concept of corporate personality,[2] answered God's call. By refusing God's dominion, he saw the dissolution of his own dominion, as Genesis teaches us in vivid language. The harmony of the human couple and its fecundity seem impaired (Gn 3:12 and 16); mutual love is changed to aversion (4:7-8); nature becomes hostile to its master and enslaves him (3:15 and 17-18). Man then discovers what he is without the life-giving breath of Him whose will he has infringed; he returns to the clay from which he was made (3:19).

The vocation that Adam and his race were unable to fulfill, Christ was to accomplish. The Saviour of mankind, He restored man's access to the Father. "Son of man," he fulfilled in His person the mission God had proposed to Adam and his descendants. Over and above this, His death and resurrection reveal the mystery for which God destined man (Eph 1:9), the mystery hidden from all eternity, because Adam was definitively only the figure of Him who was to come (Rom 5:14).

B. *Christ, the Truth of Man*

The Son of God did not come solely to reveal God, of whom He is the Word (Jn 1:1). "The man, Christ Jesus" (1 Tm 2:5), revealed what man is by accomplishing through His life and Passion his original destiny. This idea stands out more particularly from the reading of the epistles of St. Paul, notably in the passages the Apostle devotes to Christ the "last Adam" and to "the image of God."

1. *Christ the Last Adam*

The expression itself occurs in 1 Cor 15:45. It underscores the idea that Christ is the Adam of the last ages, and that He has come to establish and be the head of the eschatological community. This theme is likewise found in other passages such as Rom 5:12-21; 1 Cor 15:20-28.

a) *Rom 5:12-21*. Adam, the head of the human race, came from God's hands, bore in himself the destiny of all his descendants. He led into sin and death all those who are born of him. Like the first man, Christ Himself is head of a new humanity, and His obedience will bring the fruits which will benefit those born to this new life which His Paschal Mystery merited for the multitudes.

"Then as one man's trespass led to condemnation for all men, so one man's act of righteousness leads to acquittal and life for all men. For as by one man's disobedience many were made sinners, so by one man's obedience many will be made righteous" (Rom 5:18-21).

This obedience is the obedience of the cross, the acceptance of God's will that sent "His own Son in the likeness of sinful flesh and for sin," so as to condemn "sin in the flesh" (Rom 8:3). The obedience of Christ is the reply of the man Jesus (Phil 2:7-8), equal to the Father (Phil 2:6), to the disobedience of him who wished to be equal to God (Gn 3:5). God answered the love of His Son by "making him Lord" (Acts 2:36; Phil 2:9-11). This exaltation does not concern Christ alone as an individual person; it is the seed of the resurrection of multitudes, as is brought out markedly in 1 Cor 15.

b) *1 Cor 15*. The antithetical parallelism between Adam and Christ is adduced twice in this chapter devoted to the resurrection of the dead (20-28 and 40-48). To avoid giving here a too lengthy commentary on these pages of the Apostle, the ideas have been synthesized in an order that does not follow the Pauline text.

The first man, Adam, became a living being; the last Adam became a life-giving spirit *(pneuma zōopoioun)*. But it is not the spiritual which appears first, but the physical and then the spiritual. The first man was from the earth, a man of dust; the second man is from heaven. As was the man of earth, so are those who are of the earth; and as is the man of heaven, so are those who are of heaven (15:45-48).

Adam was created a "living soul." Of himself he is of the earth; he lives only by the breath given to him from above (Gn 2:7). Because of the resurrection, Christ escapes the earthly condition of the first Adam. In his glorified humanity He is constituted the source of life for all those who make up the race of the last and definitive Adam. In Himself He is the principle of life from on high. Henceforth He is "from heaven," that is to say, from God, even in His humanity. By His Paschal Mystery, in His body, He has drawn the world to Himself and established it in a new relationship with its Creator, founded on a new gift that comes from God, and which is God, the life-giving Spirit. Henceforth the Spirit is the life of man: it is Christ, the unique source of the Spirit: "Now the Lord is the Spirit" (2 Cor 3:17; see Jn 3:5-8).

This power of the Spirit that Christ possesses is intended for all men whom it is to draw together in love in a single body, the Church of Christ (1 Cor 12). St. Paul affirms (Phil 3:20-21) that the same spirit also affects the whole world. This idea has been clearly pointed up in a text that also follows a passage concerning Adam and Christ (1 Cor 15:20-22). For the reign of death established by Adam, Christ substitutes the reign of life that will triumph definitively "at the end": "Then comes the end, when He delivers the kingdom to God the Father after destroying every rule and every authority and power. For He must reign until He has put all His enemies under His feet. The last enemy to be destroyed is death. 'For God has put all things in subjection under His feet.' But when it says, 'all things are put in subjection under him,' it is plain that He is excepted who put all things under Him. When all things are subjected to Him, then the Son Himself will also be subjected to Him who put all things under Him, that God may be everything to every one" (1 Cor 15:24-28).

In writing these lines where he quotes Ps 8:7, related to Gn 1:27-28, St. Paul has obviously thought of the first accounts in Genesis. Christ carries out the mission confided to man by his Creator. He rules all things, even the misfortunes caused by Adam's fall, even death. All that God has given back to Him ("All things were created for Him," says Col 1, 16), Christ

restores and then submits Himself. Thus He answers the call
Adam did not understand. For this reason, raised from the
dead, like the first fruits, He will draw after Him into the kingdom those who will have received the gift of the Spirit (1 Cor
15:20-22).

2. *Christ, the Image of God*

As in the account of Genesis, St. Paul's thought is crystal-
lized around the theme of God's image.

Created in the image of God and in His likeness, Adam was
not God. Christ is the "beloved Son of the Father" (Col 1:13),
and as such He is from all eternity the "image of the invisible
God" (Col 1:15), the one in whom we may "contemplate as
in a mirror the glory of the Lord" (2 Cor 3:18; see Wis 7:26).
Christ appears, henceforth, as the truth of man, not only because He carries out His vocation, but also because He reveals
to man the eternal plan for which God destines Him. The true
image of God that man is called to show forth brilliantly is
that of the Son, that of the "man of heaven," namely, man
according to God (1 Cor 15:49). Therefore, we see how the
first creation was but the announcement of this new creation in
which it is fully carried out. Adam was but the type of Him
who was to come. Created in the image of God and the
reflection of His glory (Gn 1:26; see 1 Cor 11:7), he pre-
figured Him who would be, in the body of man, the perfect
image of God and the authentic presence of His glory. Christ
in His Person fulfilled what God willed to make of man, an
image of Himself.

In creating man to His image, God also confided to him
dominion over all things; he was to people the world in love,
and make himself the master of it. Christ the new Man brings
together all men in love (Eph 2:15) and unites them through
the Spirit in His body which is the Church (1 Cor 12). The
image of the invisible God, "He is before all things" (Col
1:17), "First-born from among the dead," and "Head of the
Church"; so that there might be established perfect Man who
realizes the fullness of Christ (Eph 2:15), He receives from
God the *"pleroma,"* that is to say, the power to take possession
of the world and reconcile to Himself all things (Col 1:19-20).

Conclusion. Christ, the last Adam, the "definitive" man, is the truth of man, whose vocation is to reproduce the image of the Son in order that He may be "the first-born among many brethren" (Rom 8:29). By His death and resurrection Christ became the new man according to God. To accomplish God's plan (Eph 1:2-14), man will have to follow the same path as his Lord and Leader. This is why man's life "in Christ" must be a "paschal" life, a daily passing from death to life.

C. *The Christian Image of God in Man's Union with Christ*

The work of grace achieved in Christ deals with a new humanity that is born in Him and develops in time and space; by baptism man receives what was won for him by the Saviour's suffering and is joined to His body, becoming a new man. This participation in the mystery of the death and resurrection of Christ is not concerned simply with the moment of baptism, but has to do with the whole of Christian life in the course of which he will be obliged to "put off the old man" (Col 3:9-10), to walk in the footsteps of Christ by imitating Him. In this way, he will make himself fit for the accomplishment of God's plan for man in this world.

1. *The Birth of the New Man*

To attain salvation, man must become like Christ in order to benefit by Christ's work carried out in his name in virtue of His title of the last Adam. This union is effected by faith and baptism.

By *faith,* because man is a spirit; and, above all, it is a question of a change in the spiritual order. It is necessary to pass from sin to the divine friendship. This demands a response from the heart of the "interior man," an answer to divine love, the principle of salvation.

"For this reason I bow my knees before the Father, from whom every family in heaven and on earth is named, that according to the riches of his glory he may grant you to be strengthened with might through his Spirit in the inner man, and that Christ may dwell in your hearts through faith; that you may be rooted and grounded in love" (Eph 3:16-18).

Faith will be man's answer to the call God sends him

through the apostolic preaching. Through the death and resurrection of His Son, God revealed abundantly (Heb 1:1-3) His plan of love for men held in the clutches of sin, shut up within themselves, and accordingly marked for death. Indeed, in Christ risen from the dead the Wisdom of God has been shown openly to men, and the apostles who were transformed by the Spirit emanating from the body of the "Lord of glory" received the mission to show forth this new life through the Word, so as to call men to share in the mystery of life which transfigures them (2 Cor 3:18-4;6). Adhering to the Word (Jas 1:18), giving one's self to God, abandoning one's self-determination, joyfully accepting to be saved through pure grace by Another, total commitment based on faith, this it is that gives access to the Father (Rom 1:17; 4:24; Eph 2:8-10,17-18).

Adherence to the Lord by faith is an integral part of *baptism* (Eph 4:5; Gal 3:26-27; Heb 10:22). It is the whole man that must be united to the Lord. Because he has a body, redemption must reach him even in his corporality; there must be a "redemption of the body" (Rom 8:23). By professing their faith during the baptismal rite (Eph 5:26; Mt 28:19), believers adhere to Christ with their whole being, for, if they unite themselves then to Christ in His Passion, they relive mystically His Passover with all its consequences; they form then but "one and the same being" with Him in His death and resurrection.

"Do you not know that all of us who have been baptized into Christ Jesus were baptized in His death? We were buried therefore with Him by baptism into death, so that as Christ was raised from the dead by the glory of the Father, we too might walk in newness of life" (Rom 6:3-4; see Col 2:12-13). The Apostle continues (Rom 6:5-11) in very studied sentences the typographical arrangement whose structure I now attempt to render. (The italicized words bring out the parallel construction of this passage conceived as a diptych.)

A a) For if we have been united *with Him* in a death like His (i.e., in baptism), *we shall certainly* be united with Him in a resurrection like His.

b) *We know* that our old self was crucified with Him so

that the sinful body might be destroyed and we might no longer be enslaved to sin.

   c) *For He Who has died* is freed from sin.

B a) *But if* we have died *with Christ,* we believe *we* shall *also* live with Him.

   b) *For we know* that Christ being raised from the dead will never die again; death no longer has dominion over Him.

   c) *The death He died* He died to sin, once for all, but the life He lives He lives to God. So you also must consider yourselves dead to sin and alive to God in Christ Jesus.

The teaching of this passage has been very felicitously brought out by Y. Trémel in these words:

> A moral perspective governs the entire passage, but the exigency of life is based on an accomplished fact, on an ontological reality, so to speak. The Christian is "in Christ Jesus"; his life, his being belong to Him. This situation is the result of a previous action which establishes this lasting result. It originates from a unique event produced "once and for all." In salvation history the decisive event is the death and resurrection of Christ. In the life of each Christian baptism is the unique act that introduces him into the redemptive mystery. To the two stages of the mystery of Christ, crucifixion-death-burial and return to life, corresponds the double aspect of Christian salvation: the crucifixion-death-burial of the old man overcome by sin and a resurrection to a new life. Through these two steps the Christian becomes "one same being with Christ."[3]

"Baptized in Christ," Christians have "put on Christ" (Gal 3:26-27) and are brought into the friendship of God because all their sins are forgiven (Col 2:13). But baptism does not only reconcile men with God, it also unites them with one another in love by suppressing the divisions that formerly placed them in opposition with one another.

"For in Christ Jesus you are all sons of God through faith. For as many of you as were baptized into Christ have put on

Christ. There is neither Jew nor Greek, there is neither slave nor free, there is neither male nor female; for you are all one in Christ Jesus" (Gal 3:26-28; see Col 3:11).

By faith and baptism the believer passes from sin to justification, from the law of compulsion to the liberty of grace; he passes from death to life. He does not escape death, but having overcome it with Christ on the cross, he is introduced into "newness of life" (Rom 6:4). The flesh is cast off, the "old man" born of Adam is put to death and buried; a new man is born in the image of Christ because he is animated by the very life of the Spirit (Rom 8:9-11). Through their union with the risen Christ, Christians are made sons of God; they share in the inheritance of life and form a new people united in love and forming the body of Christ whose vital principle is the Spirit given from above (1 Cor 12:13; Ti 3:5-6; 1 Pt 2:1-12; 3: 18-4:2).

2. *The Growth of the New Man*

Baptism is a unique action in the life of the believer and one that permits him to attain the unique action of salvation history which marks the coming of the last days: the death and resurrection of Christ. Christian life is therefore marked in its beginning by a conversion. The Christian turns away from the world of sin to become attached to Christ in His death, signifying that Christian life is marked in an indelible manner by the sign of the cross. What the baptized have become mystically, they must continue to become throughout their earthly life. "Created in Christ Jesus" (Eph 2:10), they must manifest constantly in their daily lives this creation which is not *of* this world and yet *in* this world.

The moral activity of the Christian is determined by the new *being* received through baptism. Sacramentally, the believer is dead to the life of the former world; he is born into a new life. Morally, he must make the new man grow in a slow and laborious manner (like a long "walk," according to an image pleasing to St. Paul; see Rom 6:4; 8:4; 14:15). Salvation is possessed, but in hope. The Spirit is given, but as a deposit. The new life is won, but death and resurrection are still to come (see 2 Cor 1:22; 5:5; Eph 1:14).

To the degree that the old world continues to exist conjointly with the new order established by Christ's resurrection, the former principle of sin remains in man conjointly with the new principle. The baptized must therefore reject vice, because they "have cast off the old man with his dealings"; they must practice virtue since they are "clothed with the new man." These two aspects have been joined by St. Paul in a text from which the preceding expressions have been taken, and they particularly deserve to hold our attention. The text is Col 3:5-14 of which verses 9 and 10 (italicized) form the hinge:

> Put to death therefore what is earthly in you: immorality, impurity, passion, evil desire, and covetousness, which is idolatry. On account of these the wrath of God is coming. In these you once walked, when you lived in them. But now put them all away: anger, wrath, malice, slander, and foul talk from your mouth. *Do not lie to one another, seeing that you have put off the old nature with its practices and have put on a new nature, which is being renewed in knowledge after the image of its creator.* Here there cannot be Greek and Jew, circumcised and uncircumcised, barbarian, Scythian, slave, free man, but Christ is all, and in all. Put on then, as God's chosen ones, holy and beloved, compassion, kindness, lowliness, meekness and patience, forbearing one another and, if one has a complaint against another, forgiving each other; as the Lord has forgiven you, so you also must forgive. And above all these put on love, which binds everything together in perfect harmony.

a) *Put off the old man.* In baptism the practices of the old man are put to death (see Gal 5:24). The old man is the man of the world of sin, the man under the law, trusting in himself and in his doings that are not of God, but are 'human precepts and doctrines," poor rules that parade as wisdom but indeed "have no value for checking the indulgence of the flesh" (Col 2:20-23). In baptism all this dies with one blow, and that is why paradoxically the believer must little by little put these things to death in his daily life. As the Apostle teaches, in order to keep alive this baptismal stripping in his daily life, he must "mortify" that which in itself is "earthly," and banish from his life all lying. Lying and worldly practices are the two weapons of the old man that must be perseveringly laid aside.

The practices are the adjuncts of what St. Paul calls the "members that are of earth," that is to say, those areas of the Christian's activities that have not yet been reached by the Gospel, where the breath of the Spirit has not yet penetrated. The verb "mortify" underscores the idea of the labor required for this struggle. If with a single blow we kill the whole body, by mortifying one or other member of the body we put to death the actions inspired by sin and the "flesh" (understood in the Pauline sense, corresponding to the Hebrew *basar,* that is, man considered in his weakness and in his perishable condition marked by sin). Then St. Paul enumerates two lists of vices which for him characterize the actions of the fleshly members that he brands in a general way by the idea of the lie (Col 3:9), to be taken here in a general sense: to lie is to harm, to act badly.

The *lie,* in the epistles of St. Paul, is really a synonym for iniquity, injustice, even sin (see Rom 3:7). In Rom 1:24-25, the Apostle castigates the pagans whom "God gave . . . up in the lusts of their hearts to impurity, to the dishonoring of their bodies among themselves, because they exchanged the truth about God for a lie and worshiped and served the creature rather than the Creator." The root of the lie is to be found in their refusal to establish their life on God, and by so doing they devote themselves to idols made by man, be they false gods or money, as can be understood in Col 3:6, where covetousness is called "idolatry" (see Ap 21:8). Basically, the lie is a refusal to accept the will of God: it is disobedience. On those who are factious and do not obey the truth, the wrath and indignation of God will be poured out (Rom 2:8). These ideas remind us of Col 3:5-9, where the old man is called the "son of disobedience." They fit into the context of the epistle where St. Paul intends to denounce the repudiation of God's design revealed in Jesus Christ, on the part of those who follow all sorts of rules disguised as wisdom, but which finally make them slaves of the "elements of the world" (see Col 2:20-23).

It is this lie of lying practices, of which God is no longer
the center and which "are of earth" (Col 3:2), that the believer must daily reject in order to make room for the new
man straining toward "true knowledge" (3:10), "in an élan
of submission to truth" (Gal 5:7).

b) *Put on the new man.* In contrast to sinful practices and
to lying, St. Paul defines the condition of the new man in concepts of knowledge and the image of God. Believers have put
on a new nature "which is being renewed in knowledge after
the image of its creator" (Col 3:10).

The Christian is a man in search of knowledge. This it is
that characterizes St. Paul's attitude. He presents this knowledge as the objective *(hina)* of the renewal of the baptized,
that toward which he tends and which gives meaning to his
life. The term rendered by "knowledge" *(epignōsis)* and that
could be translated also by "knowledge of a higher order,"
"true knowledge," is met three times in the early chapters of
the epistle to the Colossians (1:9-10; 2:3). It signifies simul-
taneously knowledge of God's will (1:9-10) and understanding
of His mystery and plan that Christ, the wisdom of God, obtains (2:3; see Eph 1:9-10). To say that Christ gives knowledge of the mystery of God equates the affirmation that in discovering it man is seen as revealing the love God has for him
(Eph 2:4). When he is united to Christ and shares His life,
his destiny finds its meaning, the meaning that God in His love
gave it. This knowledge is not to be thought of as knowledge
about God; it has an existential meaning for the whole man; it
demands a gift of his person to God who calls him in Jesus
Christ (1:18) and through whom he gives himself to Him
(3:19). In short, to "know God" is to let oneself be known
by Him (Gal 4:8), to concur in His plan of love, conformable
to the biblical meaning of knowing that signifies having a concrete experience of reality. Christ allows us to know God because by uniting ourselves to Him we see God and we know
His will, not because Christ would reveal mysteriously what
it is fitting to do, but because by adhering to Him we hand
ourselves over completely to God: we make Him the axis of
our lives. This is the meaning of the concept of knowledge
mentioned in Col 3:10. By baptism the Christian meets God in
Christ and dedicates his existence to Him. Knowledge is the

fruit of a "renewal" because it increases in the measure that
man lets his life be transformed by this new life, and it will
attain its fullness after death when man will share the lot of
the saints in light (Col 1:12-14). Now his life is still "hidden"
(3:3); for this reason St. Paul says that this renewal has to
do with the "interior man," the man who in his religious dimensions under the action of the Spirit (Eph 3:16) "is renewed
from day to day" in God's eyes, whereas in the eyes of man
he seems to be wasting away (2 Cor 4:16). Because Christ
lives in him through the Spirit, the baptized is nourished ("is
filled," Col 1:9) by this knowledge of Christ's love "which
surpasses all knowledge" (Eph 3:19).

It is through a renewal *"in the image of Him who created
him"* that the baptized hopes to attain this divine intimacy.
In the order of salvation, described in Col 1:15-20, as parallel-
ing the order of the first creation, Christ is the beginning, the
root (1:18). To be renewed, the Christian must bear the image
of Christ. According to the New Covenant, one can bear the
image of God only by being renewed according to Christ, the
image of the invisible God (1:15) and the beloved Son "in
whom we have redemption" (1:13-14). We see, then, the nature of the relationship that ties in growth in knowledge with
the fact of bearing the image of God. The progressive renewal
of the Christian is the function of his assimilation with Christ.
In the measure that his moral conduct is the manifestation of
the life of Christ that quickens him, the baptized accomplishes
God's plan for him. The allusion to the accounts of Genesis
is manifest. Adam had been created in the image of God.
Wishing to taste the fruit of the tree of knowledge of good
and evil, contrary to God's will (Gn 2:17; 3:6), in other words,
wishing to possess the secret of God's plans, far from having
become equal to God as he had thought (Gn 3:5), he had
been driven from Him and delivered over to sin and death.
With Christ, suggests St. Paul, man finds himself involved in
an inverse process. In Him he has life, receives the Spirit who
transforms him in the image of the Son, the reflection of the
Father. And as Christ is He in whom are found "the treasures
of wisdom hidden from the beginning," by trying to make his
life according to Christ the believer becomes a better and better
image of God and walks on through trial toward glory where

he will know God face to face (1 Cor 13:12). The perfection
of the image will have led him to the fullness of knowledge,
and grace that works in a hidden manner in his heart will
blossom in glory (see 1 Jn 3:2).

3. *Imitation of Christ*

Between the gift of grace and that of glory human life unfolds, a period for the ripening of the seed sown in the heart
of the believer. Concretely, it is by imitation of Christ that he
will, under the inspiration of the Spirit, achieve his destiny.
The golden rule for this imitation is the law of love. The love
of Christ for His Father and for men has been fully shown by
the giving of His life on the cross. The Christian reality of
men's lives must also be measured by the place love holds in
their lives, which from baptism bear the seal of the cross of
Christ. This teaching follows from the ensemble of the Pauline
epistles as well as from the whole of the New Testament, and it
is likewise the perspective of the passage analyzed (Col 3:11-
14). United in Christ, who has become "all" for them (Col
3:11), it is from Him that believers will draw the realities of
the new world. For them the putting on of the new man is,
in a certain way, being clothed in "the sentiments that are in
Christ Jesus" (Phil 2:5). Furthermore, the titles by which St.
Paul designates the Christian—elect, holy, and beloved of God
(Col 3:12)—are taken from the Old Testament, where they are
used for the people of God, and from the gospels, where they
are attributed to Christ (Lk 23:35; Jn 1:34; Mk 1:24; Lk
4:34; Jn 6:69; Mt 3:17; 17:5 and parallels). St. Paul intends to bring out the idea that Christians form an elect people,
the "Israel of God" (Gal 6:16) which is the Church, a people
that bears titles that belong by right to Christ.

Furthermore, it may be noted that all the virtues mentioned
in Col 3:12-14 are connected with mercy. Just as God is
merciful to men, believers, in order to live according to Christ,
must practice mercy so as to imitate God: "As the Lord has
forgiven you, so you also must forgive" (3:13). All these
recommendations are expressed collectively in the command:
"And above all these put on love" (3:14). Love is like a
last garment that covers all the others, makes the Christian
recognizable (see Acts 4:32), and is the source of his actions.

Love is proper to God (1 Jn 4:7-8.16), and it was by giving
His life for men that the Son, the image of the Father, revealed
to the world God's love for all. To imitate God who is Love
is to imitate Christ, to love as Christ loved (see the new com-
mandment in Jn 13:34-35; 15:12-17). For a Christian to
love God is to love as God loves, thanks to the Spirit who
brings to his lips the very cry of Jesus to His Father: "Abba!
Father!" (Gal 4:6). Thus, this love, "the bond of perfection"
and the summit of divine imitation, gives the Christian knowledge by a sort of connaturality. None but he who loves knows
what love is; this is the situation of Christians whom God em-
powers to live and to love as He lives and loves. It is only
"as they are knit together in love" that they "arrive at the
full flowering of knowledge that will permit their penetrating
the mystery of God" (Col 2:2-3).

In a world given over to sin and death, this invitation of
the God-Man of sorrows will take the form of a "walk in
love, as Christ loves us and gave Himself up for us" (Eph 5:
1-2). Baptized in Christ's death, the believer is to become
conformed to Him through communion with His sufferings
(Phil 3:10), and thus he will complete in his flesh that which
is lacking in the sufferings of Christ (Col 1:24). "For this
slight momentary affliction" is preparing for him "an eternal
weight of glory" (2 Cor 4:17). If the exterior man seems to be
wasting away (2 Cor 4:16), resurrection will mark the logical
outcome of the baptized man's docility to that Spirit who, in
him, placed in the world in a hidden manner the new man
prepared for eternal life. Resurrected, he will become in his
human completion a new creature. Even in his body he will
be light and will live by the life of Christ who will have taken
possession of him, a seed sowed in death, in order to recreate
him a heavenly man (1 Cor 15:36-49; see 2 Cor 13:4; Jn
12:24-26). On that day he will come to the complete knowledge of the mystery of God because he will be wholly renewed
in the image of his Creator (Col 3:10).

4. *Living in Christ in a World That Waits*

St. Paul does not speculate about the earth and the new
heavens. We will refrain from concluding that he is not in-
terested in the destiny of the world, for this would be to neg-

lect one of the aspects of his theology, marked as it is by the biblical concept of the world (see above), according to which the cosmos, being the dwelling place of men, shares in their destiny. According to the Apostle, the world is in waiting, and that for which it waits is the redemption of humanity (Rom 8:19-23). Other passages from the great epistles have alluded to the cosmic primacy of Christ (1 Cor 3:23; 8:6; 15:24-28), but it is in the epistle to the Colossians that St. Paul has exposed his thought most clearly (Col 1:15-20) because of his anxiety to reply to the errors that were questioning the complete triumph of Christ in favor of the elements and powers of this world (see Col 2:8-23).

It is as "Head of His Body" which is the Church that Christ unifies and rectifies the world separated from God, so that the exploitation of creation by men who make up the Church may prepare a new creation where Christ will be "all in all" (Col 3:11). Like humanity, the world is, therefore, waiting for renewal. Doubtless there is not in the world the same tension as in men. When Paul writes that it "groans," he is projecting into the physical universe the idea of the tension seen strikingly in the moral being, man. The allusion in Rom 8:22 is none the less clear, even though it is not to be overemphasized. The universe, with Christ as intermediary, is the object of redemption; and it devolves on men to be the artisans of this work by their activity in this world created by God and confided to them: "All are yours; and you are Christ's; and Christ is God's" (1 Cor 2:22-23). Accordingly, there is no question of the Christian's escaping from the world; on the contrary, he must become a part of it and use it. However, he will be careful not to forget that if he wishes by his labor and learning to subject the world, he must make his activity conformable to man's redemption, with which the redemption of the world is bound up. This is the equivalent of saying that the world ought to be placed at the service of the new life received from Christ and organized in such a way that the love of God may be rooted in the hearts of men and ordered to the glory of the Creator. All belongs to man, but it is in Christ that everything finds its reference to God. In this reference man will understand the truth and the ultimate order of the universe that has been given to him in order that he people it

and subjugate it. He must also know that this taking possession of all things will be marked by the sign of the cross, for
the world of men is rent by hatred; and sin is set against what
comes "from above." It is by dying to the flesh and by being
revivified by the Spirit that Christ has reconciled the world (2
Cor 5:19). Likewise, it is by death to the flesh and conduct
according to the Spirit that the man "in Christ" will work in
this world if he wishes to unveil its meaning and reveal to it
the love of God, who here below took on the marks of One
crucified. Baptism does not take Christians out of the world,
but buries them in it as a leaven of life; by setting up a body
(the Church) united to Christ in love and dedicated to the
love of men, they are to be witnesses to the value the universe
has acquired in the Lord, and prophets of the hope that is in
man's world, while it aspires unconsciously to the "revelation
of the Son of God" (Rom 8:19).

Chapter 3

Christian Man in Dialectic

by Edouard Pousset, S.J.

Introduction

What is man? Aristotle would reply: a rational animal. This reply is more a problem for research than the result of reflection, for what is an animal and what is rationality? Moreover, today the question, what is man, would be criticized by many as to its very root. It assumes that there is a *nature,* an *essence* of man. Many challenge this for various reasons. Whatever may be the outcome of this philosophical discussion, man has become very much of a problem. Of what value are his conscious undertakings as he reflects and searches for light, if they are secretly conducted by his subconscious?

Has he the power to act freely if the most subtle and effective conditionings are acting upon his centers of determination? In the present state of their respective disciplines the psychoanalyst, the sociologist, the cultural anthropologist, the linguist, and others oppose fixed conditions to the philosopher who continues to think that men are able to make themselves masters of their language through conscious thought, to reach an indefeasible truth and make themselves progressively free subjects in a history that has a certain meaning.

The path is narrow between confusion and the naiveté that would ignore these conditions. This is a path to be explored. The first step on this path is an act of hope; this act is born of a certitude tenuous but firm. I am not simply the perfected

toy of anonymous forces; from my very conditionings I shall
learn the difficult art of making myself a man. One takes one
step, then another, and one discovers by experience that the
terrain lends itself to insights. Since there is an understanding
of man only in his social genesis, a first part will show the
basic connections that structure this beginning; a second part
will show the different spheres of the society they generate.

The reflections which follow are dependent upon the thought
of Father Gaston Fessard, S.J. We have chosen to refer to him
rather than to draw up a deadly dull compendium of conclusions gleaned from all directions. Father Fessard does not describe psychological situations. He analyzes dialectical relationships, each one of which is simply a clue to the others in
the development that all of them together control. Thus, when
he writes that "man still dominates woman," it must be understood that this relationship of domination occurs as a
component among others in the dialectical development that
leads man and woman to their mutual recognition in equality.

A third part will explain how the experience of contingency
seen on all levels of human existence can lead to the recognition of God as principle and foundation of all that is. Finally,
we shall show how one reaches Christian experience, the
content of which we shall summarize briefly. The Christian, as
a Christian, does not live a life different from that of all men.
But he lives it in accordance with evangelical renunciation,
that is, according to the death and resurrection of Christ.

A. *Basic Relationships*

An individual exists as a human being in and through the
network of his relationships that cause him, himself, by existing,
to be in some way "all reality." This view is not an *a priori*
and gratuitous statement. It stems from a certain thoughtful
and methodical reading of human reality, even considered in
the single sphere, still very abstract, of sensory and intellectual
knowledge. Men have a call to be, each one, "all reality."
This call throbs in the heart of every human being in the
form of *universal desire,* which is not, let us emphasize, a
psychological élan, but rather the dynamic of existence.

The little child of man is distinguished from the animal by
the fact that the animal experiences specific needs leading to-

ward specific natural objects and not to others, while the little child makes a "movement to take anything he can get his hands on in order to put it in his mouth." For the carrier of this universal "negativity," the world, that is, the ensemble of nature and other individual human beings, is his world, his thing.

Stemming from this universal desire is one of the fundamental relationships among men, the dialectic of master and slave, that not so much fulfills the desire, but rather begins to make it disappear by various mediations. Brutal or cultivated, immediate or converted, this dialectic acts in all human relationships, even in friendship and love. Let us explain it briefly, without however imagining that it could be lived according to an abstract schema. It is a question of a parable. To understand it is to reach by means of images the most diverse concrete situations.

Two individuals moved by the same desire meet. "They strike each other, and necessarily begin to fight. In the deadly struggle each one is for the other only an object of the brutish desire for a fight to the finish." If the struggle ends with the murder of one by the other, there remains a miscellaneous fact without human significance: the victor remains an animal. But it may have a different outcome:

> One may be seized with anguish in the face of the death that threatens him, the other, on the contrary may be elated in the face of such a risk. It may be that the first, hypnotized by the idea of saving his life, will ask mercy with supplicating gestures. Whereas the victor will draw from the frightened eyes of the vanquished one a new sentiment, a consciousness of himself that he was not yet aware of. These eyes, indeed, reflect the image of his liberty, these beseeching gestures recognize his power to grant life or death. The real end of the death struggle rests completely on this *recognition*. Thanks to it, the conqueror awakes to the consciousness of himself. ... Thus, in order not to lose such a benefit, he grants life to the vanquished one and is satisfied to put him in chains. Henceforth, one will be the *slave,* the other will be the *master*. The latter, henceforth in his

own eyes will live *for himself,* while the slave will live only for his master, *for another.*[1]

This *master-slave* relationship is found again analogically "at the basis of all social connections." At the root of each one of them, however tenuous or conciliatory it may appear, for the individual it is always a question of his life and his liberty, because what is at stake each time is his desire to exist and to be all.

The creation of a social bond between master and slave constitutes only the first period of the dialectic at play between them. Indeed, the master's victory does not dispense him from having to eat in order to live. And "if he really wishes to gain by having a slave . . . he must feed him. Rather than growing weary in order to take care of him, it is better, evidently, to unfasten his hands, domesticate him, and gain a maximum profit, leaving to him only what is necessary for his subsistence. We then see the slave condemned *to work* for the good of his master. But to work, is to change nature, to humanize it, and in return, to be naturalized, generalized." The servile work is going to overthrow the situation regarding the master and slave and cause the former to be dependent on the latter.

In fact, the slave asked for mercy because of his attachment to his natural life and his fear of death. Now, the anguish "that the master imposes on him in order to have him obey, is going to teach him that this natural life is in reality without value to him and that liberty alone is worth the pain of living." Furthermore, the effort that keeps him working forces him to become master of himself. Finally, he becomes expert in his work and "begins to know both nature and his own powers"; he becomes *intelligent.* "In other words, it is for him that the world that is humanized and man who is generalized are born together and know each other through each other."

> The master, on the contrary, remains an animal moved by his desires, he is unaware of the human world as well as of his universal essence. . . . He can indeed continue to use the products of servile work; nevertheless, he has become dependent on his slave.

Thus, in the social life of men the dialectic of master and slave would perpetuate itself indefinitely by inverting itself and by simply reproducing itself at levels of increasing complexity, if it acted alone in a pure state. But social relationships are not reduced to contacts where each one tries to impose himself on another by brute force, the power of his mind, his tone of voice, or even a simple look. These contacts are set up by another dialectic that we must now define.

The dialectic of master and slave contains remarkable relationships. There is the relationship between man and man that is established in the struggle that we shall call the *political* rapport, and the relationship of man with nature, brought about by work, which we will call the *economic* rapport. The first is seized by the master for his gain; the burden of the second falls back on the slave at his expense. One is severed from the other without anything in the frame of this dialectic being able to overcome their opposition. Now, in real life things do not happen in this summary manner, nor do they remain fixed in these unilateral conditions.

All society, from the most restricted to the most embracing, the family, a company, the state, is set up according to political and economic relationships, overlapping one with the other and tending more or less to be ordered one with the other as a means to an end. At least, such is the truth of the matter. The dialectic of master and slave taken by itself shows us only the *appearance* of something political or economic. The seeming political relationship is the oppressive power of the master such as results from a battle unto death, and as is practiced for selfish reasons. The seeming economic relationship is the work of producing under constraint in view of material needs. As for their truth, Karl Marx, for example, reflecting on what a communist society would be, made this suggestion. Political power become "public power" loses its oppressive character because, as G. Fessard points out, "it is placed at the service of individuals associated with a view to production," therefore at the service of the economic. Inversely, the economic factor is then an association of workers "where the free development of each one becomes the condition of the free development of all" *(Communist Manifesto)*: in other words, the means of progress for the flowering of each one's freedom, expressing itself in and through its relationship with the freedom of others. Now the relationship of the freedom of one person to the freedom of another is a political relationship. Therefore, we have here the reality of the economic rapport, a means in the service of politics.

It would be an illusion to imagine that all human society perfectly achieves the *truth* of its political and economic relationships. This truth is always something to be accomplished. However, it is at bottom the principle of a permanent effort toward *conversion* that may cause the political and economic aspects to pass from the level of appearance (where the will to power and selfishness often maintain it) to the level of truth, by means of a reciprocal subordination: "political power subordinating itself to production, therefore, to economics, as economic production subordinates itself to the development of the freedom of each and all, and, therefore to politics." G. Fessard concludes: "The unity of human society and its progress are possible only to the degree that politics and economics begin a reciprocal interaction, each one becoming alternately a means and an end in respect to the other."

Thus it is that the author calls our attention to the fact that at the heart of human relationships another dialectic effects specifically the conversion and interaction of all the elements of which the dialectic master-slave produces the disassociation. This is the dialectic of man and woman, not less universal than the other and even more fundamental. In an extremely penetrating passage that has remained isolated in his work, Marx wrote:

> The mystery of the relationship of man to other human beings *(Mensch)* finds its unequivocal, decisive, indubitable, clear expression, in the relationship of a man *(Mann)* to woman, and in the manner in which their generic, natural and immediate rapport is understood. The immediate, natural, and necessary rapport of human beings *(Mensch)* is the rapport of man *(Mann)* to woman. In this generic, natural relationship, the rapport of man *(Mann)* to nature is straightaway his rapport with human beings *(Mensch),* just as the rapport of man with human beings *(Mensch)* is immediately his rapport with nature, his own natural determination.[2]

A text of primary importance, this: Marx reveals that natural and necessary point of concurrence in the double basic rapport of human reality, while everywhere else this rapport appears irremediably disconnected in the form of politics and economics.

Let us trace the schema of this dialectic of man and woman.[3] It, too, unfolds in two periods that may be called *struggle* and *work*.

First, *struggle*. It stems from the desire that urges two beings, male and female, to look for one another in order to satisfy their fundamental need, that which Marx calls "the need of man as man," a need that their *sexual* nature, when taken separately, does not allow them to satisfy directly. Although based also on the thrust of a desire that extends to the infinite, this need is very different from that which urges antagonists in a death struggle. Each of the latter sees in the other only a *thing,* an object to be appropriated, finished, denied. On the contrary, man and woman are urged by their desire to look for a *subject* in the other, the *ego* that can affirm their own subjectivity, to the degree that their accorded reciprocity ends in union.

Now, precisely so that their union may not be simply the effect of a biological attraction, but the result of a psychological choice, it is necessary that the specific essence of their desire be revealed in the course of a competition that is a genuine *love struggle*. Brutal or refined, this love struggle is essentially the reverse of the death struggle. For each partner, it is not a qustion of proving his worth by risking his life in spite of, or rather due to, mutual threats of death. On the contrary, it is a question, by means of reciprocal assurances of life, of inciting the other partner to show the worth he attributes to the other by giving himself to him. If the man and the woman succeed in giving each other a mutual and equal assurance of their gift, they can then embrace and lose themselves in an act that establishes their unity. The man *possesses,* or rather, according to the biblical expression, *knows* his wife, as the woman knows the man; and both are *born together* to a new being and to a higher unity that love bestows on them, at the same time as they appropriate each other, one the other, one *by* the other.

In the dialectic of master and slave, the knowing appeared at the end of the second period. Here, on the contrary, it takes place at the end of the first, and it is the unity of man with nature, through work. This is the first witnessing to the real and fundamental inversion that the dialectic of man and woman brings about. Let us point out also that this analysis of the love struggle does not have a less universal or a less profound truth than that which we have recognized in the death struggle. All unification between human wills, not only individual ones but collective wills also, finds its perfect pattern in this union of man and woman. Indeed, whatever may be the occasion of it or its immediate object, a "contract" or an "alliance" never brings about the unity of the "persons" in question without having been preceded by a "struggle," the objective of which is always the exchange of a promised reciprocal gift and where the virile initiative of one calls from the other the response of a feminine welcome.

As soon as the man and woman have "known" each other, the second period of the dialectic begins; and it, too, may be called *work*.

Just as the slave in the power of the master and according to his orders finds himself obliged to transform nature, so the woman, impregnated by the virile power of the man, enters into "labor" in order to bring about the design their mutual love has formed so as to give an objective reality to their unity. Truly, a very different labor from that of the slave! In place of feeling herself undone by the anguish of death, the woman sees her life strengthened by the promise of life she bears in her body. In place of having to curb her desires, contrariwise she finds them infinitely expanded. Finally, in place of giving her form to nature and of seeing the fruit of her labor taken away by the master for his pleasure as soon as it is produced, the woman gives her substance to the human being she carries for a long time in her womb and which will never be completely detached from her. However, as the uprooting of the object worked on is necessary so that there may be created the distance necessary for reflection and in order that the slave may know his generalized and objective existence in humanized nature, so is it necessary that the labor of the woman should end by a child-birth that separates from her the fruit of her womb. This is a solemn moment for both the man and the woman, for both then recognize in the child not only humanized nature, a source of joy for the master and knowledge for the slave, but also nature made as a man, where is reflected with the bond of their love the perfect unity of the dual relationship of man to man and man to nature.

The social bond that welds them one to the other henceforth is no longer simply a de facto recognition as between master and slave, nor even a recognition equal and reciprocal, but that recognition of a right objectified in a living substance that has at the same time a consciousness of itself. Their recognition attains perfection by uniting the recognition of the fact and that of their right, and by placing them in interaction. This is the *recognition of love,* born of love and generating love.

The de facto recognition is that which intervenes between master and slave by the *fact* of force that enters in. In the meeting of man and woman there is also a factor which imposes itself even if it lies in mutual attraction and not in force. They are man and woman, and these two determinants place them in a factual relationship. Furthermore, each one has a certain temperament, qualities and faults that inevitably are going to place him, under one aspect or another, in a position of strength or weakness (e.g., timidity). The fact of their mutual attraction is transformed by the play of their freedom, in a first recognition of love (the exchange of promises). This will be solidified in marriage by the recognition of rights (equality and reciprocity) that even have a juridical expression (a contract).

This equality and reciprocity are indeed the work of love, but they are not yet completely permeated by it. The perfection of the recognition of love takes place in the course of a history, one essential moment of which is the time when they become father and mother. They are then established in an equality and reciprocity much more solid and objective than that of a juridical contract, their factual differences being maintained and becoming more than ever the path of their mutual love.

In the dialectic of master and slave, the "recognition" appeared at the end of the first period, the death struggle. Here, contrariwise, it takes place at the end of the second period, that of "labor," and it is a recognition of love, whereas the other was simply the recognition of fact. Here is a new and most important testimony to the inversion brought about by the dialectic of man and woman.

Let us note again all the importance and truth of this second analysis. There is no unification of human wills either individually or collectively that does not end by a bringing forth, or birth. The agreement brought about by a contract or an alliance is expressed straightway by a collaboration that aims at bringing to light a work in which the unity of the partners is materialized. Whether it takes the form of a simple economic act, of a juridical institution, or of a "new political order," this work is detached from those who collaborated in bringing it about, and lives its own life, like the child, and becomes for its "authors" the bond that joins them in a common knowledge and enjoyment. It is the same for the most passing daily relationships, actions, or conversations to the very degree in which they are occasions for innumerable loving struggles between persons.

Here, let us stop the analyses and compare the two dialectics. All the constituent elements of politics and economics that the first presented disjoined and opposed are in the second, on the contrary, reconciled and unified. Here, man still dominates woman, but the exercise of his power obtains immediately the good that is common to both. The woman also transforms nature, but her work produces, no less immediately, a new freedom which, as soon as it appears, establishes that society dreamed of by Marx, in which "the free development of each one conditions the free development of all." In the child, the fruit of "possession" and of the reciprocal "knowing" of man and woman, "existence is at the same time community." Achieving in this way at an embryonic stage the interaction of politics and economics, the man-woman dialectic is the exact counter-charge to the master-slave dialectic that puts them in opposition.

What is more, the first establishes the explanatory value of the second, as it alone also reveals the manner according to which the social and historical progress of human reality may be accomplished. The man-woman dialectic is the very form in which there can appear the unity of opposites of which the master-slave dialectic explains the origin. Presupposing the "immediate, necessary and natural" unity of the dual rapport of man with man and man with nature, it is the *condition for the feasibility* of any split between these terms; and by its development, it is at the same time the *topical condition* for their reconciliation since it reveals that same unity once rendered *mediate, free,* and *genuinely human,* in short, spiritual. Also, still present in each one of the disassociated terms, such as master and slave, it acts in them, without their perceiving it, so as to direct their struggle toward its solution. That is why the slave is not the only one who makes progress. While he, for example, becomes a serf, a subject, a citizen, the master for his part becomes a lord, a prince, the state. ... We shall have to see the form that the rapport man-woman takes in relation to the principal stages in the genesis of humanity. But from now on, beginning from the first stage, it appears that this rapport is in some way the *module* of the *dialectic conversion* that each time permits the overcoming of otherwise unsolvable divisions.

B. *The Spheres of Human Society*

The fundamental relationships that tie together the two dialectics of man and woman, of master and slave, produce the diverse spheres of human society. The first of these is the family:

> The concrete genesis of humanity is not brought about without these two dialectics producing a continual *interference* or *contamination* of the two movements proper to them. ... Now, a quite simple analysis will show that the necessary result (effectively reached at the end of how many millennia) of this contamination is to objectify the recognition of love between man, woman and child under the form of three new relationships, *paternity, maternity, fraternity.* These relationships by degrees are going to allow it to develop boundlessly. The father, indeed, is still the master whose power is placed naturally at the service of the familial community so as to safeguard its existence. The mother is still the servant, but the servant-wife who directs the economy—the "law of the home"

—and orients it spontaneously towards the development of liberty and the education of the children. Finally, while the multiplicity of brothers and sisters extends in a certain way the specific unity of the couple of which they are the fruit, their fraternity overcomes little by little the sexual division of their very flesh, as the *universal prohibition of incest* testifies, and it begins to open and generalize an equal and reciprocal recognition that already existed between father and mother, finding at the same time, in its original unity, the ontological basis for going beyond the recognition of rights toward a recognition of love which embraces all the members of the familial community. Paternity, maternity, fraternity, these are three essential pivots of all human society. Thanks to them, politics and economics can be related in groups extended even more widely.[4]

The second sphere of human life is the economic society, the relationship of man to man by means of man's rapport to nature (work, production of goods, exchange, distribution). Economic society is even rooted in the first relationship of man and woman in the family, but it is developed according to its own dynamism and its own structures that are not a simple extension of the dynamism and structures of the familial being.

Man here universalizes himself by becoming naturalized, whereas, inversely, nature is humanized by work. Nevertheless, the mediation of work does not really produce the synthesis man-nature. It is never only an abstract human nature that man objectifies in the universe in the manner that scientific and technical reasoning abstracts human nature. Furthermore, the individual who by work has to show objectively his own social and universal existence is not directly in contact with this, his universal and social entity. To pass from himself as an individual at work to himself as a "generic" being—that is, as a human, universal being or as a society actually existing and still to be promoted—he needs a mediator who points out to him what this universal, social being is and who makes it present for him so that he will promote it. This mediator is political power that defines, at a given time, what the common good is in a given society, that is, what the individuals at work may achieve of their own universal and social existence. Politics is already at the root of human work in the form of the constraint that the master exerts on the slave; but this is only the appearance of politics. Politics is met with again at the end of an analysis of the most elaborated economic society: public power in the service of man at work; and this is the truth of politics. This idea may be brought out in another way. A technical analysis of economic processes, of speculation and the possibilities shown for the future, brings out the fact that economics is not complete in itself, in an autonomous rationality. The politics of economics is decidedly politics; the technical analysis of the conditioning and possibilities goes back to choices that technology cannot bring about. The choices depend on man's decisions and, consequently, on politics.

The third sphere of human existence is political society. "The category of master reappears there in the state and establishes its power of constraint. Nevertheless, paternity does not stop acting in order to change this power of oppression into public power. Furthermore, *fraternity* imposes on the state as a norm of the law it promulgates, the equal and reciprocal recognition of which it is the type, and what is more, it gives the people the form of the ideal it is to pursue. Finally, the *Mother-Fatherland*, by becoming little by little the *Nation*, plays for the people the same role played by the woman in the heart of the familial community." Through many conflicts the people become the Nation, which makes its members aware of their unity with one another and with nature (the earth of the fatherland). Pursuing the role of the mother between the father and brothers, the Nation carries out the same mediating function between politics (namely, the *State*) and economics (namely, the *Society* established by the members of the Nation in relation to work).

"But this unity of politics and economics in the heart of the Nation is still only a particular unity. There are several nations and politics and economics, relationships in themselves universal, appearing then as two opposing ways by which each nation tends towards the unity of humanity."[5] The national and international developments of political and economic relationships have brought humanity, through all kinds of contradictions, in the direction of a state of interdependence that is as it were the symptom of a planetary unity, yet to be produced.

C. *The Experience of Contingency*

This interdependence among nations makes the present rending of humanity into rival groups more acute. Discord is the most universal contradiction that wages war in the heart of humanity. The world and man are contingent; they themselves are not their own origin; and they are, therefore, finite. The human being has experienced finiteness since the dawn of history; he discovers it in a simple meeting with his equal. Each one is for the other a boundary, that which leads to a confrontation in violence, evident or disguised. Finiteness must not be confused with violence, but it is the condition that makes violence possible. Violence entered into human relationships, and men do not find in themselves the principle for its definitive conversion to reason. Even in the dialectic of man and woman, which is moreover a dialectic of reconciliation, each partner still remains somewhat tempted by a threatening violence by reason of the simple fact of the boundary that each one is for the other. And even when, through happy love, they succeed in mastering their ambition for power and their appetite for enjoyment, they still have to accept the suffering of being exterior, one to the other, each one in a finite state. But this finiteness may be for them the very way that will lead them to recognize in their milieu the presence of God, origin, bond, and end.

In economic and political society, the inconsistencies that affect and reveal human finiteness are no less glaring. They culminate in the tensions that reign among nations and the conflicts that rend them at times, incapable as they are in overcoming their desire for power and in regulating the disputes that oppose the common good of each one to the common good of all.[6] A thorough examination of life and the meaning of such conflicts would permit the discovery of the contradiction experienced by all at the level of world history, contradiction still admitted by philosophers, although generally in a more abstract manner, existential contradiction *par excellence,* that is, the fundamental contingency of the world and of man in the world. Even if fearful historic conflicts would find their solution either by the worldwide establishment of a society of plenty, or by a universal extension of socialistic systems, man would not be spared the experience of his own finiteness and contingency; this experience would be painful in proportion to the success it would imply in the order of the rapport of man to man and of man to nature.

Taken in its metaphysical significance, this experience of contingency would become the sign of a necessary going beyond the horizon of the human world by an affirmation of the absolute as a basis, at one and the same time transcendent and imminent, of the unity of man with man, and of man with nature. Then from a metaphysic of the absolute, experience and human reflection would pass into the realm of religion. Finally, in religion, reason would discover the place, the role, and the unique meaning of the historical religion of a God made man.

Coming back then to the problems that arise concerning the situation of men and their international relationships, one would not find it difficult to discover their import and to suggest a solution for them:

> Under the species of economic and political supremacy, in reality, for man it is a question of his attitude *vis-à-vis* the All of being, that is, God. Because of his will for power (expressed in politics), man aims at absolute transcendence, at being like God. Whereas, by his appetite for pleasure (that he tries to satisfy by economics), he dreams of an absolute immanence, a being which would be the world. To place these two opposing attitudes in interaction and in order that human unity may be possible, (it would be necessary to note) that there is at work here a dialectic between the All of being and man, analogous to that of man and woman: *the dialectic of God and humanity.* Present in us, and therefore interior in relation to those dialectics that develop in temporal events, this dialectic also directs them and becomes at the same time the principle of a new genesis of humanity, a genesis, still historical, although no longer simply natural, but strictly speaking, *supernatural,* and truly spiritual.[7]

The religion of Israel and Christianity are the revelation of this dialectic.

D. *Christian Living*

Life according to faith in Jesus Christ begins by an experience of the Holy Spirit, as it did for the inhabitants of Jerusalem who listened to the apostles on the morning of Pentecost. Already a simple question about the meaning of life proceeds from such an experience. No one comes to God, even to God as reason may recognize Him, without having been enlightened and drawn by God's action in the depths of his heart. To ask oneself about the meaning of life is to have been prepared by this action. *A fortiori* the man who believes in God and who still seeks Him, only comes to Jesus Christ when he is impelled by the Spirit. This visit of the Holy Spirit may take very different forms: a meeting, a word heard, a book read, an act of charity of which one is a witness, or a beneficiary. . . . Finally, whatever it may be, it puts the man who receives it face to face with a fact, as unimpeachable as it is inexplicable, and closely or distantly it concerns the existence of Christians in the world, that is to say, of the Church. In presence of such a fact there is a great temptation to reduce it as much as possible to some accepted good so that it will no longer give rise to questions. The witnesses of Pentecost did just this when they considered that "these men were full of new wine" (Acts 2,13); with a witticism they rid themselves of an awkward problem. However, those who let themselves be summoned by this unimpeachable and inexplicable experience question the Church in the person of one of its members who makes them realize the facts by referring it to the history of Jesus. For all facts relating to the existence of Christians in this world have their origin in Jesus Christ. "Men of Israel: hear these words, Jesus of Nazareth. . . ." Such is the beginning of Peter's discourse in response to those who were astonished at what they saw on the day of Pentecost (Acts 2:22).

He who seeks God is then placed in the presence of the "fact of Jesus," and a precise field of research is opened to his reason. This research is possible, for Jesus of Nazareth furnishes its subject heading. It is addressed to the intelligence of the people of Israel in virtue of the long history it had experienced, and what it says to them is addressed through them to the intelligence of men of all times. In the course of its history the people of Israel had formed a certain idea of God, of itself, and of life; it judged the works and words of Jesus as a result of this experience. Those who became disciples concluded that He was indeed the Messiah; and because of some of the happenings (death and resurrection), they understood that this Messiah was the very Son of God.

Their reasons for believing can become the ones adduced by whoever feels himself challenged by an irrefutable fact regarding Christian life today. His quest leads to adherence; he enters into a life governed by faith. Within the faith he continues to be nourished by the Word of God; he becomes familiar with the Scriptures and from them learns what Christian life is. The Gospel alerts him to the subject of the Kingdom of God brought to us by Jesus Christ, and which, henceforth, "is among us."

The Christian cannot fail to note the challenge the Saviour proposes in behalf of the Kingdom: "For there are eunuchs who have been so from birth, and there are eunuchs who have been made eunuchs by men, and there are eunuchs who have made themselves eunuchs for the sake of the kingdom of heaven. He who is able to receive this, let him receive it" (Mt 19:12). This is a declaration in which Tradition, in the light of the Master's example, has recognized a call to celibacy.

"If you would be perfect, go, sell what you possess and give to the poor . . . and come follow me" (Mt 19:21): a call to poverty, which under this form seems limited to some who are invited to make themselves free in order to follow Jesus as messengers of the Good News. This call has a warning about riches that concerns everybody: "How difficult it is for those who have riches to enter the kingdom of heaven!" (Lk 12:33). And finally it speaks to all: "Sell your possessions and give alms" (Lk 12:33).

Finally the disciple of Jesus is introduced to the heart of the mystery of the Son of Man when he hears that he who wishes to be the first will make himself the slave of all. The mystery of the Son of Man is to do the will of His Father: ". . . I seek not my own will but the will of Him who sent me" (Jn 5:30). Now, the will of Him who sent Him is that the Son give His life for a great number: "For the Son of man also came not to be served but to serve, and to give His life as a ransom for many" (Mk 10:45). He calls to serve as He serves, in obedience to the Father, to become the slave of all, as He who, "though He was in the form of God, did not count equality with God a thing to be grasped, but emptied himself, taking the form of a servant, being born in the likeness of men. And being found in human form He humbled Himself and became obedient unto death, even death on a cross" (Phil 2:6-8). "And Jesus called them to Him and said to them, 'You know that those who are supposed to rule over the Gentiles lord it over them. But it shall not be so among you; but whoever would be great among you must be your servant, and whoever would be first among you must be slave of all" (Mk 10:42-44).

Reflecting on this triple call, the Christian cannot but recognize there the very charter of his paradoxical life. By chastity, poverty, and humble service of his brothers in obedience to the Father he lets his heart be reached by evangelical self-sacrifice and by Christ's death; thus dying with Christ, he is risen with Him. There is no category of Christian life that is not already a category of human life; there are no structures of Christian life that would not already be structures of life common to all. The Christian, as a Christian, tends simply to live, according to a modality proper to him, the life of all men. He lives it according to the death and resurrection of Christ.

We have seen that man manifests himself and becomes a living man according to a triple dynamism that develops in three essential activities and produces human society:

1) The loving desire that inclines the human being toward his counterpart: man toward woman, and woman toward man. This desire is the origin of conjugal and familial society.

2) The power of taking possession of the natural universe that is an extension of his body. In the measure that by work he begins to possess the world, man consolidates his individuality and constitutes economic society: production, exchanges, appropriation, consummation.

3) The will to independence, whereby man affirms his liberty in presence of his counterparts and his power to conduct himself by reason. He assumes responsibilities and exercises authority in view of the common good. This will is the origin of political society.

Three passions and three sins may issue from these three

urges when they become unruly: carnal lust and lechery, the thirst for riches and selfishness, and, finally, the will to power and spiritual pride.

By recommending renunciation, the message of Jesus not only aims at these three capital sins, but also goes to the heart of our existence in the areas of natural goodness, in order to make us go beyond ourselves toward Love which is the life of the Holy Trinity. Chastity is a renunciation which renews the heart for the love of God and all creatures. Poverty renounces the possession of goods and thus introduces a new relationship to the world's riches. Obedience is a renunciation of one's own will which favors adherence to the will of God and entrance into true freedom.

This Christian life according to the evangelical call is death and resurrection, life through death. The Christian who lets himself be seized by this mystery experiences little by little how liberating this death is and finds the path to a harmonious life. In each of its spheres human life is indeed marked by contradiction. In the relationship of man and woman, the antinomy of love (selfish will of the good of the other) and of desire (that contains a selfish will of possession for oneself) is only solved with difficulty and never definitively so long as God is not recognized as the concrete bond of those who love each other. In the economic sphere, in view of the endless complexity of the avenues of exchange, and the desire for pleasure that falsifies all processes, productive work may end, and in fact does end, in disorder and frustration. As for the political sphere, in nations and among nations, there are violent contradictions. These have their source in the will to power of each one and the incapacity of all to resolve the conflicts that oppose the common good of each one to the common good of the others. Now life according to the Gospel, for all those who have the experience of it in their lives, is a progressive resolution of life's antinomies and the very fulfillment of its values by means of a certain type of renunciation conducive to an immediate realization of them.

Indeed, by opening up to the perspectives of love in perfect chastity, life according to the Gospel progressively resolves the persistent antinomy that undermines the relationship of man and woman in relation to sexuality. By a call to poverty that strips of all for a total gift of self to God, one is liberated from the appetite for pleasure that urges unbridled production and the avid possession of riches in the economic sphere. Finally, by a call to humble service according to the Gospel, Christian life cuts at the root the undertakings of the will to power.

It is not a question of drawing straightway from the Gospel a "Christian political system" or an economic system. It is a question of experiencing in everyday life the liberty of the risen, even if institutions resist the law of death and rebirth which is the condition of this liberty.

The liberty of the risen! The Christian then experiences the greatest joy of loving as Christ loved, of being poor and of serving. He is poor, but he possesses the earth. He no longer has a will of his own, but God personally does for him all he wishes. He seeks solely the Kingdom of God and His justice, but the rest is given to him over and above. This is how man becomes man!

Conclusion

In the pastoral constitution *Gaudium et Spes,* Vatican II proposed to all men a definite anthropology on the level of reason and on the level of faith, and it pointed out the great human tasks of our times. The intention of the Council was a pastoral one, and its teaching is not cast in a systematic form. Nevertheless we find in it, particularly in the second part, the essential structures by which man becomes man by creating society.

This second part is announced in modest terms: "Some questions particularly urgent in these times." In fact it handles problems that deal with essential points of human life: marriage and the family, culture, the economic and political spheres.

What is man? "O eternal God, it is in your nature that I shall know my own nature."[8] In any case it is not necessary to seek to answer this question fully. Nevertheless we can determine definite lines of action based on our knowledge of the essential relationships which make up our existence. In this way, starting from the conditions of our lives, we can become all together a bit more human, that is to say, more free and more true, with others and with God.

Part Two

Interior Man

by Andre Derville, S.J.

(unless otherwise noted)

Introduction

"The interior man" and "the exterior man" are expressions that belong to the Christian vocabulary since the time of St. Paul. We plan to make a survey as to the meaning of these words as used by some authors who are particularly important within the Christian tradition. There is no attempt to make this survey exhaustive. Furthermore, our research will be limited to the study of explicit uses of the expression and will not take into consideration equivalent expressions.

As is evident, this meaning—or these meanings, for the uses made of "the interior man" by the same author are not always consistent—is often related to the author's concept of the structure of the soul and of the process of man's divinization.

Chapter 4

Saint Paul

In Scripture, only St. Paul uses the expression "interior man," and that three times. Before defining its meaning, one ought to note that the gospels recount teachings of Christ in which is found the distinction beween the interior and exterior of man (e.g., Mk 7:21; Mt 6:4 and 18; Lk 11:39). Moreover, the commentators of the three Pauline texts that speak of the interior man (*ho esō anthrōpos*) pay particular attention to recognizing this expression or others close to it in anterior and contemporary literature.

Thus Plato speaks of *ho entos anthrōpos* who battles those wild beasts that are bad instincts,[1] and intends therefore a clear meaning of interiority, of moral conscience.[2] It is the same for rabbinical literature, and in Philo, in hermetical texts, and among the stoics; later, Plotinus will speak of the interior man in two important passages.[3] E.-B. Allo thinks that this expression goes back to an idea common among the thinkers of the hellenistic world already at the time of St. Paul.[4]

Without discussing the question of knowing where St. Paul found the expression "interior man," we shall try to define the meaning he gives to it from the contexts where it is used:

Rom 7:22: "For I delight in the law of God, in my inmost self, but I see in my members another law. . . ."

Eph 3:16: "that the Father according to the riches of his

glory may grant you to be strengthened with might through his Spirit in the inner man. . . ."

2 Cor 4:16: "So we do not lose heart. Though our outer nature is wasting away, our inner nature is being renewed every day" (the expression *exterior man* which is here opposed to *interior man* is a hapax in Scripture).

A. *Rom 7:22* occurs in a passage about the division of man (7:14-25), generally interpreted as describing man under the empire of sin, not yet justified and renewed by the Spirit. His division, his powerlessness, consists in this, that he is divided between the law of God and the law of reason on the one hand and on the other by the "law of his (carnal) members" and the law of sin (vss. 22-23). The interior man takes pleasure in the first two and undergoes the slavery of the two others. Let us note that St. Paul does not say, nor does he imply, that the exterior man takes pleasure in the law of the flesh and in the law of sin. He is satisfied with showing the interior man as that part of the "natural" man that is in harmony with the Spirit and the divine law, with his higher faculties of correct judgment and moral conscience which are sensitive to the true and the good. Governed by reason *(nous)*, he has a heart inclined to the fulfillment of the divine will and submits with joy to its authority. According to St. Paul, the new man, the new creature, is quite something else; here we might characterize him as an interior man freed from divisions, regenerated, inhabited, and transformed by the Holy Spirit (see Rom 8).

B. *Eph 3:16.* The first part of this epistle explains the mystery of salvation given in Jesus Christ, the new Man whose mystical Body integrates all the members of the house of God. It is in the prayer that concludes this section that the expression "interior man" appears. Here Paul does not show him as in Rom 7, given up to division, but already living by the Spirit, the mystery of salvation. The meaning of verses 14-17 suggests a double movement, first descending from the Father toward man, then going up from man to the Father. From the Father comes the gift of the richness, the glory, the power (biblical terms with similar meaning when applied to God). This divine gift through the Spirit is given to the Christian "according to the interior man," and we may think that Paul explains what he means by this when he continues: "that Christ may dwell in your hearts through faith" (vs 17a). From now on, the interior man becomes the spiritual man with a believing heart, established in love, and becomes capable of grasping and knowing what the love of Christ and the fullness of the Godhead are (vss. 17b-19); such is the ascending of man toward God.

In this profound passage, which is interpreted in many ways because of different possible grammatical constructions, the interior man means man considered in his most deep personal interiority, where the regenerating Spirit moves him, where Christ dwells through faith and where is born the love that comes from Christ. Therefore the expression is taken in a sense at the same time similar and different in Rom 7 and here: similar, because in the two passages it is a question of that secret and intimate part of man, the part that is spirit, open to God; but from different points of view. In Rom 7, the interior man is divided, with his spirit powerless against the flesh and sin. He is polarized and held captive by his very struggle on the level of the flesh and sin. But in Eph 3, liberated by the Spirit, the interior man is called to penetrate all the dimensions of the mystery of God. This seems to signify that the reign of the Holy Spirit in the new man causes him to take possession of higher or deeper areas of his "interior man," areas that are inaccessible so long as he is not morally regenerated.

C. *2 Cor 4:16.* Here again, Paul speaks of the interior man who has become spiritual, and he does so in an eschatological perspective. He distinguishes him from the exterior man "who is wasting away in ruins." For St. Paul this exterior man expresses not only the body, but all that is connected with the life of this "psychic" body, the whole domain of exterior activity, the relationship with the visible and concrete world (see vs 18), everything about the human person that is visible to the eyes of others. Here the interior man is on the contrary the one whose spirit is "renewed from day to day" and already grasped by invisible and eternal realities.

This passage suggests a double movement, simultaneous and
inverse, of diminution and increase that evokes Phil 2:7-9
("Christ emptied himself ... became obedient unto death. ...
Therefore God ... exalted him"). Indeed, the apostle sharing
in the mystery of Christ reproduces with the same richness in
his own life the passing of Christ from this world to His Father through death (2 Cor 4:7-15). In the passage under consideration, the interior man does not evoke to a great degree a
part of the soul, and the distinction between the exterior man
does not refer primarily to a difference of level of interiority.
It is a question of the apostle's personality "seen from the outside or seen from the inside," living *in via* the regeneration of
the new man.

We see that in the three cases analyzed above the Pauline
expression of the interior man admits shades of meaning required by the context. It has nevertheless a fundamental, con-
stant meaning, that of man as spirit with his faculties, which at
the level of personal conscience put him in touch with the true
and the good. In this contrast with the exterior man there is no
dualism. For Paul it is the whole man who has become the
old man, the carnal man, because of sin, as it is the whole man
who is called to become a new man, a new creature through
Christ and in Christ. It is in the interior man that are found
the secret associations with God's salvific plan. It is also in
the interior man that faith and life according to the Spirit
begin to show themselves and with them, therefore, regeneration and salvation. Let us note, finally, that Paul does not
compare the interior man and man created to the image of
God; Origen will make this comparison.

Chapter 5

The Patristic Age

To illustrate the patristic age, we are choosing, first, Origen (†c. 253) as the leader of an important theological and spiritual school of thought, particularly in the East, then John Cassian (†c. 435), as representing monastic spirituality, and, finally, Augustine (†430) as the father of Western spirituality.

A. *Origen*

Origen rather frequently employs the expression "interior man." It is used most often in the context of his theology of man created in the image of God and particularly in the texts where he comments on the double account of creation or refers to it. For example, in the prologue to his *Commentary on the Song of Songs,*[1] this double account is interpreted in the light of the Pauline doctrine of the interior man.

The interior man indicates the place of *kat' eikona,* that is to say, the superior part of the soul, the seat of the *logos* (reason) peculiar to each one, with its faculties of knowledge, of judgment, of moral good, and, in its highest area, the seat of *nous* (*mens,* intelligence), which is under the influence of the divine *Pneuma:* "It is in the interior man where are contained the seat of virtues, the totality of intelligence and knowledge, that the renewal of the image of God takes place."[2] When he is regenerated, the interior man becomes the new man, no longer carnal, but spiritual, the image of God.

In the work of Origen, the most highly developed passage on the interior man, and also one of the most synthetic regarding the different aspects of his spiritual anthropology, is the second part of the *Discussion with Heraclides*.[3] There he presents and applies the principle of the analogical structure of the two images: "Just as the exterior man has for a homonym the interior man, so it is with his members; and one may say that each member of the exterior man is found again . . . in the interior man."[4] Therefore, we have here one of the foundations of the doctrine of the spiritual senses and of the allegorical interpretation of Scripture. To these two levels in man, exterior and interior, correspond two lives, carnal and spiritual; two intelligences *(psyche* and *nous); two loves *(eros* and *agape).* "In Origen the whole range of human operations will undergo this law of division in two which will echo the theology of the visible and the invisible."[5]

The vocation of the interior man is to become a perfect Israelite, that is to say, according to the etymology of the word *Israel,* capable of seeing God.[6] For man the sinner, "the renewal of the interior man in so far as he is reasonable and intelligent, consists in the knowledge of God and the indwelling of the Holy Spirit."[7] All therefore must work to find in themselves the interior man, following the example of the woman in the Gospel (Lk 15:8) who sweeps her house to recover the lost coin.[8]

If we admit the authenticity of two datable fragments of the fourth century published by F. Diekamp,[9] Athanasius of Alexandria (†373) employs the theme of the interior man and the exterior man. In a doctrinal context, moral rather than metaphysical, he establishes a perfect parallelism between the two men, each one endowed with five senses. The other activities or properties of the body become in turn symbolic of the activities or properties of the interior man. This doctrine likewise allows Athanasius to understand symbolically the language of Scripture, such as "O taste and see that the Lord is good" (Ps 34:8). These two fragments are very close to Origen's *Discussion with Heraclides.*[10]

B. *John Cassian*

In the preface to his *Conferences,* Cassian indicates the relationship between this work and his *Institutes* in this way: "Let us therefore pass from what is visible to the eye and the external mode of life, of which we treated in the former books, to the life of the inner man, which is hidden from view..."[11] In fact, the *Institutes* deal with the activities of monastic life and the monk's exterior combat with the capital vices. This combat is basically the asceticism that imposes on the body and the whole exterior comportment of the monk the discipline capable of regulating them. By contrast, the *Conferences* regularly lay stress on the spirit animating the monk, on his thoughts, desires, and affections, on the purity of his heart; and they deal with progress in the spiritual life properly so called.

In the various passages where Cassian uses it, the expression "interior man" refers essentially to "the one who gives himself to the wholly interior struggle against the evil thoughts" of the heart.[12] The expression is not explicitly defined or explained from the viewpoint of spiritual theology, nor is it integrated into a comprehensive doctrine on anthropology that does not exist for this author. It is always distinguished from what appears on the outside, to the glance of others, from that which can be controlled from the outside; in this way it keeps a fairly definite meaning. It seems to come naturally to the pen of Cassian and is to be understood easily by his readers as showing a fundamental distinction between two areas of spiritual combat.

In the case of the abbot Serenus, "the vice of impurity was dead in the inner man; he wished now that this death would extend to the exterior man" to the point of his being no longer subject to the physical movements of the flesh.[13]

"But if any one strike you on the right cheek, turn to him the other also" (Mt 5:39): this other cheek is not the left, as an exegete would think. For John Cassian, "let the interior man also turn the right cheek to be struck by humbly consenting to the affront.... For the interior man must not be disturbed, even silently, because of a blow received by the exterior man."[14]

C. *Augustine*
by Aimé Solignac, S.J.

A complete study of the Augustinian concept of the *homo interior* would require broad developments. It is one of the central points from which the whole thought of Augustine could

be understood. Here it will be sufficient to point out the sources
of the doctrine, to establish its major orientations, to present a
group of texts (not exhaustive) and a concise bibliography.

In this area Augustine underwent a double influence, neo-
platonic first of all. In Plotinus he read that the One, the intelligence, and the Soul are in us, that is to say, in the interior
man *(ho entos anthrōpos)*.[15] In Porphyry, perhaps in the treatise
On the Precept "Know Yourself" and in the *Return of the Soul,*
surely in the *Aids to the Study of the Intelligibles,* he found the
idea that man must enter into himself to escape indigence and
effusiveness in multiplicity, and in this way unite himself to
Being and to the All.[16] It is this neo-platonic influence alone
that is present in the writings of Cassiciacum.[17]

But after having read the *libri platonici,* Augustine begins
the reading of St. Paul.[18] Very quickly the neo-platonic themes
of recollection and union with spiritual realities combine with
the Pauline themes of the new man, reformed in the image of
God.[19] As soon as he returns to Africa in 389, the drawing up
of the work *On Genesis against the Manicheans* leads him to
comment on Gn 1:26. He interprets this text in order to refute
the Manichean accusation of materialism, by saying that man
made to the image of God is to be understood as the interior
man.[20] During the same period, *The Teacher* affirms that
God is to be sought and prayed to "in the secret parts of the
rational soul, which is called the interior man,"[21] and to support
this he quotes Eph 3:16-17. With the same meaning, but with
more stress on neo-platonic inspiration, is to be understood the
famous text in *De vera religione*: "Do not go outside yourself.
Return into yourself. Truth dwells in the interior man."[22]

The predominance of Pauline themes is affirmed on the
other hand in a synthetic text of the *83 Questions.* We know
that these "questions" are a resumé of the discussions held
at the monastery of Suk-Ahras and date from the years 388-
391. In *Question 51* Augustine, on the basis of 2 Cor 4:16,
asks himself if it is the interior or the exterior man who is
made in the image of God (Gn 1:26). The answer has subtle
variations. While giving his preference to a solution favoring
the meaning of the interior man, Augustine endeavors, nevertheless, to show that the exterior man is not a stranger to the
divine resemblance. Every creature bears a trace of the

divine goodness that made it, the human body more so than material beings because it possesses simultaneouly existence and life. The human body is subject to the spirit: man's upright posture is a sign of this superiority by comparison with the body of animals and of this adaptation to the spirit, since it makes man capable of contemplating the sky and superior realities.[23] But the interest of *Question 51* is that it is in direct line with the thought of Paul, the *interior man* being placed there in relationship with the renewed man, opposed to the old man (Col 3:9-10; Eph 4:23-24), and the heavenly man in the image of Christ opposed to the earthly man resembling Adam (1 Cor 15:49). Furthermore, the interior man coincides with the *spiritual man,* for man alone by his spirit *(spiritus* identical here with *mens)* is truly in the image of God and adheres directly to Truth.[24]

As we see, Augustine from then on gives the preference to a theological and ethical interpretation (the renewed man opposed to the old man), without renouncing a metaphysical interpretation (the interior man as a locus of truth, with soul and spirit; the exterior man as body). The doctrine of *Question 51* will be handled by him again, point by point, during his mature period, around 415, in *On the Trinity.*[25]

A complementary aspect of the Augustinian *homo interior* is its connection and even identification with *cor,* which for Augustine is the innermost center of the person, the point where all his powers meet and from which radiate all activities, the place where God is found and joined to us, where He is loved and tasted.[26] The heart, understood thus, and it is the biblical meaning, is the very dwelling of interiority. Just as the exterior man can by the bodily senses arrive at corporeal realities, the interior man can by the feelings of his heart, or spiritual faculties, arrive at spiritual realities and God Himself who is their zenith and source.[27]

The interior man, then, is for Augustine authentic man, man at his best, his highest and deepest. By this return to genuineness, man is linked immediately to spiritual realities. Discovering thus the characteristics of his divine Prototype in whose image he has been created, man is enlightened by transcendant Truth which rules his thoughts and is moved by Love which inspires and governs his actions. While concentrating thus on himself and on God of whose presence he is aware, man is not shut up in a deceptive solipsism or exclusive theocentrism. The authentic meaning of creation and the meeting with the Creator send him back to the whole of creation, and to the world of men in particular, although these aspects are not explicitly included in the idea of the interior man.

Chapter 6

From the Middle Ages to the Sixteenth Century

A. *The Twelfth Century*

We shall limit ourselves simply to William of Saint-Thierry, some of whose writings have been widely circulated under the name of Saint Bernard, and to Richard of Saint-Victor, a good representative of the Victorine school.

1. *William of Saint-Thierry* (†1148)[1] presents a general view of the spiritual life according to three degrees that are most clearly expressed by the words "animal man," "rational man," and "spiritual man." These expressions are essential to his thought, and they habitually retain the same meaning. This is particularly evident in *The Golden Epistle to the Carthusians of Mont Dieu.* It is in this context that William uses the expressions *homo interior, homo exterior.* Of themselves they do not have any meaning in the spiritual order, but are part of William's way of seeing the structure of man.

The *homo exterior* is an expression that synthesizes that part of the soul called *anima* which is linked to the body, moves it in all its activity and is dependent on it. The *homo exterior* is a given that spans the whole of human life, while the *homo animal*[2] expresses the state of infirmity, blindness, and powerlessness of the man who is still a slave to his body, his senses, his passions, and who has not yet become either rational or spiritual.

As for the *homo interior,* it is the part of the soul called *animus* which is connected with invisible realities and with the spirit *(intellectus, mens).*

In the lowest state, called "animal," the exterior man, supported by a simple faith and led by obedience, is formed according to a pattern of action for the active life, in a struggle to repress vice and acquire virtue. Thus exercised and directed, the *homo animal* accedes to "the substance of the interior man."[3] The *animus* is then by study and meditation on revelation to be subject to the light of faith, to seeking knowledge of the truth and the desire of good. *Animus* is the faculty that moves the *homo interior*; and William defines it as the place for the renewal of God's image: "in the interior man is that likeness by which man is renewed from day to day through the knowledge of God, according to the image of Him who created him."[4] The progressive restoration of the image in the interior man (see Gn 1:26, the first account of creation), and the birth of the *homo rationalis* are not yet his vivification by the divine breath (see Gn 2:7, second account of creation), and the birth of the *homo spiritualis.*[5]

This third stage of spiritual progress which man can only prepare for and desire is completely due to the gratuitous gift of the Holy Spirit. The *homo spiritualis* is born and develops in the interior man. The knowledge of the rational man becomes wisdom. The good that he wished for is given to him in love. In the *intellectus* of the man who has become spiritual, there is awakened what William calls a "greater and more noble sense of understanding."[6] This sense of the spirit is directly inspired by the Holy Spirit.

The expressions *homo interior, homo exterior* are again used by William on the subject of the different degrees of knowledge of the Holy Trinity,[7] in relation to the spiritual exegesis of Rom 7:24-25,[8] and in order to explain the repercussion of love and divine wisdom on the action, the countenance, the body, and the senses (glorification of the *homo exterior*) of the spiritual man.[9] In these passages William remains faithful to his idea of three stages or spiritual states in man. We know that his doctrine as well as his formulation of it are inspired by Origen, and also his explanation of the spiritual senses.[10]

2. *Saint Bernard* (†1153) rarely uses the expression "in-

terior man" and does not give it any appreciable prominence.[11]

3. Richard of Saint-Victor
by Robert Javelet

The writers of the school of Saint-Victor love that play of dialectic that distinguishes, in fact opposes, the two ways or the two poles of the activity of the spirit, that which is exterior *(foris exterius, extrinsecus . . .)* and that which is interior *(intus, interius, intrinsecus . . .).* Above all, Richard of Saint-Victor presents a coherent doctrine on this subject. One would find the elements of it more in William of Champeaux (†1121) than in Hugh of Saint-Victor (†1141). Regardless of the personality of the author of the *Questions on the Epistles of Paul* (the pseudo Hugh) the definitions he gives are valuable for the Victorines: " 'The exterior man' regards what we have in common with the animals; 'the interior man' what we share with the angels. 'The old man' includes both aspects, for not only 'the exterior man' but also 'the interior man' are old because of sin."[12] Therefore, interiority is not spirituality in quest of self and God; it is a human reality that may be good or bad. If we wish to form a judgment about it, let us open "the mouth (or desire) of the interior man" and ascertain if he "hungers for carnal and temporal things or for spiritual and heavenly things."[13] Likewise, the work of the exterior man may be good or bad.[14]

Interior man corresponds to *cor,* to what is invisible and what is solidified in man through *mens*: "The mind *(mens)* is the principal faculty of interior man."[15] This *mens* apprehends its relationship to objects proper to it through what it sees in visions, as the head of the exterior man apprehends through sight the appearance of the visible world.[16] "The interior man has two eyes. . . . One is the eye of discretion, the other the eye of circumspection."[17] We know the importance Richard gives to discretion, symbolized by Joseph: "Our Joseph should know as fully as possible the total state and disposition of the interior and exterior man."[18]

What discretion reveals and, if necessary, governs is the excellent harmony between the exterior and interior man. The reciprocal knowledge, activity, and influence of the two are such that the normal perfection of one requires that of the other, a perfection that the resurrection will render definitive.[19]

The harmony between the exterior man and the interior man is analogical; there is a hierarchy: "Invisible realities are within; visible realities are without. Therefore what is invisible is above; what is visible is below."[20] Here, discretion is replaced by wisdom which reads in *(intelligere)* exteriority the sign of interiority. "Notice how the state of a man is described for you in terms of the comportment of the exterior man."[21] There is no question of a single comparison; the harmony that unites the exterior man (together with the visible world) to the interior man (together with the invisible world) has the power of a symbol.[22] The exterior man's second manner of vision "is an overflow from the power of a heavenly sacrament" ("intus magna mysticae significationis virtus continetur," *ibidem*). And so the noetic approach conformable to this existential harmony is an *investigatio*. It is in the third kind of contemplation that the hinge joining the exterior man to the interior man is best shown; the first serves as a "guide" for the other, like Eve for Adam.[23]

There is sin when the hierarchical harmony is disturbed and meaning abolished. Mortification consists in putting the exterior man in his place.[24]

If the exterior man shows a trace of the interior man, the latter is, through the *mens,* the image of God. Henceforth the spiritual life will demand not only the quieting of the exterior man which must not block the thrust of the interior man toward God, but also the sleep of the interior man in the *excessus mentis,* at the time of the division of the *anima* and the *spiritus* by the sword of the divine Spirit.[25]

B. *The Thirteenth Century*

With the flowering of scholasticism the vocabulary becomes more definite and specialized. Like many of the other expressions in the patristic tradition that had their origin in Holy Scripture, those such as the interior and exterior man are no longer part of the thought patterns used habitually by the scholastic theologians. When they do use them, very often it is because they meet them in St. Paul.

1. *Saint Thomas Aquinas* (†1274), in the *Summa Theologica,*[26] is opposed to identifying *homo interior* and *anima*. The *homo interior* is the *pars intellectiva* and is distinguished from

the *pars sensitiva cum corpore* of the exterior man. Once he has made this distinction, he reverts to his usual vocabulary. In his commentaries on St. Paul he does not fix his attention on the passages that speak of the interior man.[27] Let us note that these same commentaries offer developments on *homo carnalis* and *homo spiritualis;* the latter is defined thus: "that part of the soul . . . which . . . by the Spirit of God is enlightened in the intellect and inflamed in the affections and the will."[28]

2. In *Saint Bonaventure* the Pauline expression is likewise rarely used, and as in Saint Thomas, rarely a dominant theme. Even in his specifically spiritual works, he uses habitually *anima, mens, cor,* rarely *homo interior.*

In his *Commentary on the Sentences,* however, he defines *homo interior*: "Paul calls the rational spirit itself the interior man since by means of it man occupies himself concerning heavenly things. . . . The (interior) man possesses powers of the soul by means of which he is turned toward spiritual things."[29] In his sermons, the opposition of the two terms sometimes appears.

Without using the term "interior man," the *Breviloquium*[30] presents a double structure in man; he is endowed with two senses, "interior and exterior, of the mind and of the flesh," which are ordered to a knowledge of the "interior book" and the "exterior book" (Ezr 2:9; Ap 5:1) of creation. The interior book opens to the interior sense and reveals to it Wisdom, the invisible, spiritual, and eternal realities. Without using the term "interior man," Bonaventure then explains how the creature always mounts up to God in three ways: by the traces of God found in the universe, by being His image because he is an intelligent being, by being in His likeness when he is just; these determine three sorts of conformity with God: inferior, interior, and superior, and three sorts of vision of God: fleshly, reasonable, contemplative.

Therefore, in Saint Bonaventure as in Saint Thomas, the interior man is not the object of any theological or spiritual reflection, even slightly developed. It is not a part of any of their categories of thought.

3. *David of Augsburg* (†1272), a contemporary of Bonaventure and like him a Franciscan, has left us *On the Behavior*

of the Exterior and Interior Man (ed. Quaracchi, 1899) that
was widely circulated, if we are to judge by the large number
of manuscripts that have come down to us. The nature and
content of this work have already been shown.[31] Here it suffices
to remark that in the first part, *"For Novices on the Behavior
of the Exterior Man,"* as in the second part, *"Formula for the
Reformation of the Interior Man,"* the term we are studying
is used infrequently. When it is used, its general meaning, as
in other places in the same work, is close to what we have
said in reference to John Cassian. First, and above all, it pro-
vides a convenient distinction.[32]

C. *The Fourteenth Century*

Along with representatives of Rhenish mysticism and that of
the Netherlands which had considerable influence on Christian
spirituality in the following centuries, we find spiritual writers
who give evidence of an earlier tradition. For example, Henry
of Friemar, the elder, a hermit of St. Augustine (†1340), com-
piled the two great works of John Cassian in his *On the Spiritual Perfection of the Interior Man.*[33] His confrere Hermann
of Schildesche (†1357) organizes his *On the Cloister of the
Soul*[34] in two parts, one on the *homo interior,* the other on the
homo exterior. If the influence of Hugh of Fouilloy (†1172/
74) is evident in this work, it seems that Hermann thinks of
these two expressions as did David of Augsburg. But these
unpublished works are eclipsed, particularly if we judge them
in the perspective of time, by the powerful syntheses of an
Eckhart or a Ruysbroeck.

1. *Eckhart* (†1327/28). For Master Eckhart, the part of
man, the "place" where his divinization occurs, the center of
his unity with God, are defined by two equivalent expressions
according to the essence of the reality they express. In the
first place the *Grund der Seele,* the depth of the soul, generally
retains a meaning sufficiently exact; and it has been handled
in detail.[35] The second expression is the interior man, *inner
Mensch,* that admits of many shades of meaning, depending on
the context where it is found.[36] It is in the interior man that
the Father engenders the Son, that the image of God is restored,
and that unity and equality with God are established. The *inner
Werke,* the interior work, is the part man plays in his diviniza-

tion. It does not consist in virtuous exterior actions, but in a tendency, a yearning, and ultimately in an adherence in faith to God present in the interior man. In practical spiritual life, the believer, according to the measure of his progress and the birth of God in him, enters into the depths of his being and according to that same measure, is there more united to God. For Eckhart, all this is presented as a possible experience, at least in his writings of a non-speculative nature. He even speaks of this interior work as a permanent state of adherence to the Divine Being in interior nakedness. To explain it, he compares it to the natural and permanent weight of a stone, whether it falls or remains motionless.[37]

The spiritual teaching of Eckhart on the interior man is above all presented in the treatise *The Aristocrat,* the treatise *About Disinterest,* and two Latin sermons.

However, Eckhart still uses the term "interior man" in his more speculative works. In the frame of his apophatic theology, he quotes the "Do not go outside yourself; return into yourself; in the interior man dwells Truth" of St. Augustine,[38] using in a significant way 'God' *(Deus)* instead of Truth *(Veritas).* While Augustine oriented the believer to the interior man so that he might there meet God as Truth, and in this manner grasp what he is, Eckhart follows Denis the Areopagite[39] and his negative theology. It is not so much God as Truth that the interior man will meet, but the presence of God as Being "in the intimate and highest recesses of the soul itself." It is existence *(esse)* that is intimate with God and in which man participates, and "it is in this manner that he must seek for God, who remains the hidden God *(Deus absconditus)* for as long as He is the *Esse.*"[40] If the divine Being is inexpressible, unnamable, He is not unknown to him who seeks Him; there is a hidden relationship between God and the human creature.

This relationship is not found in the exterior man. ("To the outward man belong those things that depend on the soul but are connected with the flesh and blended with it, and the co-operative functions of the several members...")[41] nor is it found even on the level of virtuous actions, but at the root of man's existence. Therefore, it is by a return to his inner depths that man approaches the mystery of the Living God.

Moreover, certain texts of Eckhart clearly establish the interior man even in God: "In no way is he in time or in place, rather he is in eternity. There is God and only God, there God rises because there He is ... There the interior man is most expansive with a greatness other than physical magnitude." He is an essence sharing the divine essence, and we may wonder how it may be attained by a living man *in via,* who is far away from the eternity of heaven, existing as he does in the region of contrast *(regio dissimilitudinis).*

On another level we find the same pattern of thought and the same distance, when Eckhart speaks of the interior Word and the exterior Word of God. The interior Word is the Son, produced by a divine act inseparable from God's essence and without which God could not be what He is. By this act, He expresses and says perfectly what He is. The exterior Word is the created world, a sort of exteriorized version by which the Father permits an exterior view of something of that which He is.

In Eckhart there is a sort of analogy, of identical structure, between the relationship interior man—exterior man and the relationship interior Word—exterior Word. Because God does but one thing, there is therefore a relationship between the interior Word of God and the interior man, a relationship that the theology of the image of God renders comprehensible. This relationship, this analogous structure, is on an ontological plane, and such theorizing could not satisfy the mystic who is seeking God, because it allows the distance and the radical dissimilarity between God and the creature, His external work, to remain. Grace alone abolishes them. Why can man *in via* receive this grace? The answer is found in the Incarnate Word who unites in Himself God's interior and exterior work, the eternal and the temporal, the uncreated and the created. How can man *in via* live this grace? He receives it in the depth of soul, in his interior man, who passes thus, if we may so express it, from the power to act to the act.

This presence of God in man operates first and essentially in the deepest part of his being, beyond the level of the powers or higher faculties; justifiably, it grants the soul "union with God, life in and with God." Its first effect is to reorganize interiorly man's relationship with God, then through man's virtuous cooperation to change him in relation to his higher faculties and, finally, to make his lower powers submissive to the higher ones.

In the meantime, through the progress due to grace, the exterior man, while remaining in time and in an inevitable dissimilarity, redirects himself to God by his works. The interior man, reprieved, lives by God alone, dwells in eternity, enters into a resemblance with the interior Word of God, and becomes one with and equal to God. All these expressions refer to one and the same reality, divinization. Only in glory does this divinization take over the whole man, but it is already found in the interior man since he has his roots in God. Outside of this secret point of contact, into which he would be able to penetrate only by a mystical experience, the believer must be satisfied with an *a posteriori* knowledge of God, beginning with his external works, a knowledge, still insufficient, distorted, unsatisfying, of the "One whose name is above every name."

According to these few indications, we note a variety of meanings in the use of the term "interior man." Let us say, in short, that in Eckhart's more speculative works, he has a tendency to place the interior man in God, to identify him with the divinized man, while in his works more directly ordered to a practical spiritual life, the interior man comes to birth through a search for God by detachment, humility, an interior stripping, and is strengthened in his interior adherence and submission to the will of Him who is in him.[42]

2. Both *John Tauler* and *Henry Suso,* disciples of Eckhart, use the term "interior man" only rarely, but then with reference to the spiritual life.

Thus, Tauler in his sermon 15,[43] and in chapters 27 and 30 of the composition known as the *Institutions* of the pseudo-Tauler, shows a few points about the structure of the human soul; in these texts we find the terms *homo internus, exterior homo.*[44]

3. *John Ruysbroeck* (†1381)
by Albert Ampe

In his works, Ruysbroeck uses readily and without previous justification the terms "interior man" and "exterior man," which correspond to the terms "interior life" and "exterior life." He gets them from a long patristic, monastic, and scholastic tradition built on the Pauline notion of the "interior" man, both in psychological and spiritual speculations of varied origins and from the experience of spiritual persons and the mystics. As for himself, Ruysbroeck gives these terms shades of meaning, which vary within the doctrinal and lived synthesis of his complex spirituality, according to multiple considerations of a theologial, psychological, and spiritual nature.

Indeed, this spirituality considers man placed in his diversified relationships with the cosmos, the exterior world, and with God. This dual rapport that man is to integrate harmoniously in the development of his personality, one and complex, does not imply a dualistic view of the universe, but brings out the basic complexity of a concrete reality that makes man a dweller on the confines of two worlds. In Ruysbroeck's perspectives that are deeply Aristotelian, although sometimes expressed in Platonic assertions, basically man is composed of body and soul, through which he comes in contact with the "exterior" world and with God.

a) The exterior man. For Ruysbroeck the exterior world is the whole universe, whose existence is bound in matter and which is being developed by humanity. It involves the order of nature and super-nature. In it a transcendent God became incarnate and His presence is prolonged in the Church in order to form His mystical Body and transform humanity through faith and the sacraments which in their significative materiality bring grace. It is in this vast exterior world that the exterior man must define his attitude; his spirit involved in matter, dependent on it and called upon to organize it, he must recognize this world as established by God. He must use it *(uti)* for God's glory according to His commandments and those of the Church. In this loyal attitude, with regard to the conditions proper to this world as well as to the law of his human nature and the exigencies of the divine transcendence, he recognizes God as the first principle, the supreme regulator, and the last end. Thus, human activity in the world is penetrated and dominated by this view man has about God, and which is the principle of his morality. God is present in it, since He is there adored in humble service and obedience as its principle and regulating master, and with an upright intention is recognized as a last end.

b) The interior man. Furthermore, by his spiritual openness to God, man in his own "interior" may reach God as the object of his spiritual activity. In the interior life, God is recognized, no longer as the ruler of an activity concerning the world, but as the proper object of the spiritual faculties of knowledge and love. This differentiation of the two "lives" implies that this activity is not at first moral, but ontological and psychological. Indeed, the virtuous man may not withdraw himself from his duties in the world; he must rather integrate this world in such a way that he retains all his spiritual liberty so as to be involved equally in divine perspectives, and this by being joined to God as the end itself of his spiritual activities. Exterior life is blameworthy only if it is vitiated in itself or if it remains bound by an unlawful and selfish attachment, which is what constitutes sin.

In an interior life, man must develop his union with God. Ruysbroeck presents this union as a complex ascension with multiple aspects. Beginning with the unity of his lower faculties (unity of the "heart") that finds God in the material world through a subjectivity mixed with feelings, man is raised to the unity of his higher faculties which reach God in relative independence of matter, in order to enter into essential union. In this union, God unites Himself directly to the very essence of the soul in its highest receptivity, which is at the same time the supreme activity of the spirit.

In this interior life, the object of which is God, one will distinguish, therefore, two major degrees of union with God, according as the soul is united to God directly or indirectly.

Whereas the term "interior life" receives its fundamental meaning by its opposition to exterior life, according to our definition, Ruysbroeck, while limiting its area of application, also uses it to designate an indirect union through successive phases. He reserves the term contemplative or divine life for essential, direct, union,

e) This spirituality is evidently marked by *introversion,* in the ontological sense of the word. Indeed, there is a progressive spiritual interiorization by a return to oneself, by a gathering in of the faculties, with the attention directing them toward a center always more personal and receptive, and by a rising (or descending) toward God present in the depths of one's being (essence, in the meaning of Ruysbroeck). Nevertheless, if this introversion is expressed in psychological terms that recall intellectual, Platonic, or other speculations, it is done concretely under the influence of grace, in a climate of spiritual purification and under the effective impulsion of love, which is developed in the essential antitheses of humility and liberty.

Moreover, introversion always calls for its complementary aspect that impels the man united to God to give himself to His service with all his human powers in a "common life," a progressive synthesis, yet never completed, of action and contemplation. Ruysbroeck expresses this ideal in the prologue to *The Sparkling Stone:* "The man who wishes to attain the most perfect state within the holy Church must be a zealous and virtuous man, a man spiritual and interior, a man raised to contemplation and an ordinary man turned towards the world."

This perfection is achieved only by a generous effort, constantly renewed and directed toward an unattainable goal. "In this union between God and the soul, the desire (of progressing) is stirred up and urged each time toward new interior acts, and by this activity the soul rises indefinitely towards a new union. Thus the activity and the union are renewed unceasingly along with a renewal of activity and union. This is what the (interior) spiritual life is."[45]

4. *The Imitation of Christ.* Considering its very great influence, let us note that the *Imitatio Christi* uses the term "interior man" only rarely. When it does, it has ordinarily a general meaning, and in short refers to the man recollected within, in the presence of God, there where Christ comes to visit him, in the place from which the man may approach the "interiora Jesu Christi." In this respect, a good example of the doctrine of the *Imitatio* is chapter one of the second book (see also chapters five and six: "To walk with God within, and not to be held without by any affection, is the state of the interior man"). In one passage the interior man is related to the image of God: "Therefore, as nature is kept down and subdued, proportionately greater grace is infused; and every day by new visitations the interior man is remade according to the likeness of God."[46]

D. *The Sixteenth Century*

1. More directly dependent on John Ruysbroeck and an

important link between him and the French spirituality of
the seventeenth century is the Benedictine *Louis of Blois* (†
1566).[47] In the preface to the most doctrinal of his writings,
the *Spiritual Institution,* published in 1551, he takes care to
present briefly the structure of the soul such as he considers it
in his teaching:[48] the *anima,* properly so called, with its exterior senses (corporeal) and passions; the *spiritus,* with its
three powers that are like "spiritual" senses; finally, the *mens,*
"the apex of the spirit, Godlike ground of the soul, the soul's
simple essence, marked with the image of God." After which
he remarks that the scriptural terms *homo interior* and *homo
exterior* come within this schema; exterior man refers to the
body and to the lower powers of the *anima* (passions) which
are dependent on the body for their operations. The interior
man refers to "the depths of the soul with its higher faculties."
However, these expressions are scarcely used by Louis of Blois
in his work.

2. Without delaying here, let us point out a few authors of
great importance in spiritual and religious history who have
used the terms we are studying.

Didier Erasmus (†1536), in his *Enchiridion militis christiani,*
speaks of the interior and exterior man in reference particularly to St. Paul whom he interprets very liberally. We perceive
in his text clear connections with allegorical exegesis after
the manner of St. Augustine or St. Bernard. He equates the
interior man with the spiritual man, the new man; and the exterior man with the carnal man, the old man. These terms
have for him a meaning that at first is spiritual. Then Erasmus
explains his concept of man's structure (flesh, soul, spirit [*caro,
anima, spiritus*]) by invoking the authority of Origen.

Chapter 7

Seventeenth-Century France

A. *The Success of the Word "Interior"*

Already met in the sixteenth century, the success of the word "interior," used as an adjective or a noun, becomes extraordinary in the seventeenth century.[1]

1. At this period, everything becomes "interior": the term becomes a part of everyday language along with the vagueness this entails. It seems that the term we are considering, "interior man," when it is met, places the stress on the interiority of the moral and spiritual conscience, and because of this, it takes on a very comprehensive meaning. It seems to mean the equivalent of the spiritual man, the Christian on the way toward perfection, the man of prayer. But more or less it still suggests a major characteristic: the Christian of whom it will be said that he is an interior man, is he who is committed to an interior religion by the practices of introversion.

Nevertheless, an attentive study of the doctrine of one or more authors who use our term with some precision and constancy would reveal the nuances and the fitting characteristics they give it. Later, we will attempt this study in the works of a few of the spiritual writers. This does not prevent our stating that at this period the term "interior man" has, above all, a general and ordinary meaning.

2. First, here are a few titles of works where our term appears. In them it has only a very vague meaning, and often it is not even used in the body of the book.[2]

3. On the other hand, we note that the *theologians* of as-

ceticism and mysticism do not use the idea of the interior man. This is the case with the great Carmelite theologians. When James Alvarez de Paz (†1620) uses it,[3] he does so with the meaning of John Cassian, whom he quotes. But these expressions are above all handy distinctions, and he scarcely adverts to them in the body of his work. The mortification of the interior man will be studied from the angles of self-love, of self-will and judgment, of the passions, of thoughts. Surely, in a manner very different from that of the Carmelite theologians, Jean-Pierre Camus (†1652) shows his concept of the soul's structure without resorting to the distinction between interior and exterior man.[4]

4. Among those who are preoccupied with defining the *vocabulary* of earlier spiritual writers, the Jesuit Maximilien Sandeus (†1651), in his valuable *Key to Mystical Theology*,[5] studies the various meanings of the term *homo interior,* particularly among the Rhenish and Flemish authors. He will not be imitated by his confrere, Antoine Civoré,[6] nor, later, by the discalced Carmelite, Honoré de Sainte-Marie.[7]

B. *The Theme of "Interior Man" in Some Spiritual Authors*

After these general remarks we will show how a few *spiritual writers* use the idea of the interior man.

1. For the Recollect, Maximien de Bernezay,[8] "the very name of interior man, that the Apostle used and that we still use today to express the purity of the Christian life, shows sufficiently that we have never distinguished ... the interior man living within himself in the spirit and life of Jesus Christ, from what we call the Christian man."[9]

In the first chapter, Maximien insists, the exterior man "is called the old man by Saint Paul, the man of sin, the animal man ... the slave of his passions and senses; the interior man ... is called the man of heaven ... the new man formed on the idea of the new Adam who is Jesus Christ ... animated by His spirit and interiorly living of His life; in a word, the interior man is such a complete image of Jesus Christ that he expresses in himself all the features of Christ's perfections."[10]

2. While Maximien de Bernezay and Boudon have scarcely any concern about explaining clearly for us the structure of the soul, the discalced Augustinian from the Province of Dauphiny,

Alippe de la Vierge Marie, is careful to do so in the beginning
of his work.[11]

In corporeal man the soul fills the triple function of giving
him vegetative, sensitive, and rational life; "but beyond this
interior and natural life which consists of the operations of the
soul, there is another that is interior and spiritual" and "by
which he knows and loves God." "Indeed as the soul is the
life of the human body . . . in the same way . . . God is the
life of the soul. It is very true that man separated from God
and deprived of grace does not stop living a natural life interiorly and exteriorly because he has his soul; but, nevertheless, he cannot be called an interior or spiritual man, in as
much as God has withdrawn from him."[12]

This accepted, it follows that the interior man, understood
thus, must take as his model in the spiritual life the life of
God according to the example revealed to us by Jesus Christ
(*Discours* 2 and 3). We see that for Alippe, the interior man
is man formed according to Jesus Christ and living by His
life and Spirit. One of the interesting features of his work
is that he stresses well that all activity, all the circumstances of
human life, even the most material, must be lived and animated
by this "interior man" (see the 94 practices proposed in the
third part). In this respect Alippe differs from many of his
contemporaries for whom the Christian spiritual life seems
limited to prayer and other devotional exercises. God, the life
of the soul, must permeate the whole man through the operation of his soul; such is the interior man.

3. More interesting for our investigation, because more
coherent, is the doctrine of Jean Aumont.[13] The "poor villager
without science or study other than that of Jesus crucified"
seems to have been acquainted with one or the other text of the
Rhenish or Dutch mystics.

He devotes a few pages to an explanation of man's structure.[14] He is made up of two parts, "one exterior and material,
as is the body, and the other, interior and spiritual, the soul. . . .
Each of these two parts has in it two subordinated levels (exterior senses, interior senses or passions, on the one hand;
spiritual powers and the center of the soul's substance, on the
other). And God being the center of the substance of the soul,
the bodily senses are consequently the farthest from God, being

the surface circumference and the most distant from the divine center because of dissimilarity."

Moreover, his work is presented as the progressive deliverance from seven slaveries. After sinful actions and attachment to earthly goods come the attachments to the pleasures of the external senses, the interior senses (passions of the soul), to the independent proprietary use of the powers of soul, to one's own life. These four slaveries correspond exactly to the four levels of man. The seventh slavery is an attachment to divine gifts which are given in the substance of the soul.[15]

In all this, there is scarcely any question of the interior man. However, Aumont frequently uses the term in the course of his work to have it indicate the center of the soul. "We are Christians only in the measure that we know how to converse in our interior with Jesus Christ, our dear Exemplar."[16] The world of grace being the heart and interior of man, it is by the heart and the deep interior of man that it is necessary to go to God for God."[17]

At other times, by a slip from container to the contained, Aumont goes so far as to write that the interior man is the depth of the heart with Jesus Christ,[18] that the interior man is the man from within, "the new man . . . it is Jesus Christ and in him, the whole man renewed,"[19] that Jesus is "the interior of his interior man,"[20] that "the Divinity has made itself the center of man."[21]

For, "if you wish to know the place destined for his Majesty to bring about all these marvels, it is the depth of your heart through which you must pass to the dead heart of Jesus in order to enter finally into the living heart of His Divinity, the divine center of your spiritual center."[22]

Therefore, the man without God is a soul scattered outside its center, a soul without center or without life and, from that time on, his "interior man" is, on the metaphysical plane, but an empty frame and on the spiritual plane only nothingness.

4. Jean-Joseph Surin (†1665) does not use the terms "interior and exterior man" in his chapter on the "Economy of the Soul."[23] On the other hand he uses them in his description of the "true interior."[24] In this text Surin states "three things proper to the interior man": a) to have little esteem for exterior things; b) to have much occupation and exercises within

one's self, in the interior faculties of the soul, such as attention to the presence of God, to interior movements, as "some labor or undertaking for the regulating of the soul"; c) to remain with God in the interior dwelling. This latter has lower and higher levels, the highest and most noble of which is the innermost or the center of the soul.

Nothing reveals any originality on the part of Surin in his use of the interior man. The term, moreover, is not used frequently in his work.[25] We must say the same for Louis Lallement, Surin's master,[26] and the latter's disciple, Jean Rigoleuc.[27]

François Guilloré (†1684) draws a portrait of the interior man according to the model of Christ in the Blessed Sacrament.[28] He develops the following characteristics: recollection in the solitude of the heart, "spirituality" (the spirit rules the body, the senses, and the passions), the destruction of self-love, union, "indissoluble, delightful, dependent, and secret," with God who is the life and last end of the soul.

Among these few Jesuit authors whom we have just quoted, the interior man is the object of descriptions. This term points out the Christian who is advancing on the path of perfection in the spiritual life by the means offered by introversion. For John Nicholas Grou (†1803), we find a meaning slightly different. The Christian must be an interior man, because the Gospel demands from the disciple of Christ something over and above the exterior observance of the commandments, the gift of his heart, an upright intention, an adherence of his person to the person of Christ.

Conclusion

At the end of this investigation, and taking into consideration the shades of meaning proper to each author, it seems that the term "interior man" has been used by spiritual writers with meanings and in modes that admit a dual classification.

A. The first category is based on the greater or less exactitude of the term. For John Cassian and David of Augsburg, the exterior man is man such as he appears and acts exteriorly; the interior man is the thoughts, sentiments, and desires, all that is invisible to the eyes of others. The two terms are in opposition to each other, as the within and the without, the invisible and the visible. The distinction is elementary, handy, and practical; it is prompted more by common sense than by any philosophical or theological concept.

For the majority of the French spiritual writers of the seventeenth century, the interior man can be considered the equivalent of the man of prayer, the new man, the spiritual man. The "exterior man," which term is used much less frequently, is understood at times as sinful man, the old man, the carnal man. This dual meaning that cannot be recommended as coming purely and simply from St. Paul, is particularly evident in the works of Maximien de Bernezay and Boudon. In the same way, there will be a tendency to identify the interior life and the spiritual life. These uses of language, in themselves, give the idea that progress in the spiritual life, in the perfection of Christian life, is closely dependent on progress in interiority and introversion.

For the majority of earlier authors, the *homo interior* has a more definite meaning, depending on their idea of the soul's structure.

B. At this point the second category appears with its claims. In the uses to which it is put, the "interior man" has either a spiritual or a metaphysical meaning.

For the spiritual writers of the seventeenth century, of whom we have just spoken, the interior man refers most frequently to the spiritual order. On the contrary, it has a metaphysical meaning in the definitions given it and the uses made of it by William of Saint-Thierry, Richard of Saint-Victor, Thomas Aquinas, Louis of Blois. The "interior man" is, then, a concept that expresses an integrating part of the soul's structure, whatever may be the differences in representing it.

Let us note that Origen, possibly, and surely Augustine use the idea of the interior man in its two meanings, spiritual and metaphysical. They can be distinguished according to their context. As for Eckhart and, in a certain measure, for John Ruysbroeck, their philosophical, theological, and spiritual concepts are so synthetic that it would be hazardous to place them without fine distinctions in our classification. Their thought tends to present man and his spiritual perfection as an identical and unique reality.

Finally, it may be asked whether the metaphysical concept of the interior man, an integrating part of the soul's structure such as we see it used by certain Christian authors, may be found again, but with a different vocabulary, in modern philosophy.

For the latter, within the realm of psychology, we will qualify as being interior "all that exists in so far as known consciously or which is relative to consciousness."[29] Lalande qualifies as exterior "that which appears to have an existence independent of the knowledge we have of it."[30] In this meaning, all that affects the psychological consciousness, ideas, sentiments, and so forth constitutes the first and most superficial level of interiority.

But man, by his intelligence and deep affectivity, has a way of acting upon these interior data and exterior objects. He has the power to be detached in relation to them, to make them relative, to judge them, to use them, to go beyond them; in short, he enjoys the freedom of reflection, of choice, and of action vis-à-vis his interior world. This freedom describes a new and second level of interiority, deeper than simple psychological consciousness. It is the level of reflection, deliberation, and judgment which are exercised in relation to the true, the good, and the beautiful.

However, this more interior level is not yet that of our being and our liberty of spirit in their root. Our being and our freedom are not identical with our reflection which deliberates and judges, even if it is through our reflection, that is to say, indirectly, that we succeed in putting them together and expressing them to ourselves within certain limits. The "depth of the soul," as certain spiritual writers say, is not in the nature of psychological or reflective consciousness, and yet it is that which in us is most ourselves. It is there that God dwells. Modern authors would designate this level as the most interior one of the human being by using the term *existence,* existence at its ultimate source, beyond consciousness.

It is in this general framework of the three major levels of interiority that it is necessary to situate today the *interior man* of the spiritual writers. For them this term refers first of all to the second level. None of them places the interior man on the plane of simple psychological consciousness. Therefore, we should be careful not to interpret it on the psychological level, or with an introspective meaning (introspection being the simple observation of a consciousness by itself). For them, to speak of the interior man is, definitively, to point toward the most intimate level, the deepest center, the depth of the soul, where man is called to fix his dwelling place in order to unite himself there to God present and to live his whole life of action and contemplation in subjection to the Holy Spirit. This orientation is consonant with the Pauline doctrine of the interior man, even if it does not recapture all its shades of meaning.

Notes*

NOTES TO CHAPTER 2

[1] For the gospel data, see the art. "Évangile," DS, vol. 4, cols. 1747-1772.

[2] See J. de Fraine, *Adam and the Family of Man* (New York, 1965).

[3] Y. Trémel, "Le baptême incorporation du chrétien au Christ," *Lumière et vie* 27 (1965) 88.

NOTES TO CHAPTER 3

[1] G. Fessard, *De l'actualité historique*, vol. 1 (Paris and Bruges, 1960). For the explanation of the *master-slave* dialectic we quote excerpts from pages 142-146. The same texts will be found in the articles published in *Recherches de science religieuse* 35 (1948) 31-38.

[2] K. Marx, *Oekonomisch-philosophische Manuskripte aus dem Jahre 1844* in *Marx-Engels-Gesamtausgabe*, 1. Abteilung, vol. 3 (Berlin, 1932) 113. In French: *Manuscrits de 1844* in *Oeuvres completes de K. Marx*, ed. and trans. E. Bottigelli (Paris, 1962) 86.

[3] See Fessard, op. cit., vol. 1, 163-170.

[4] Ibid., 170-171.

[5] Ibid., 171-172.

[6] See G. Fessard, *Autorité et bien commun* (Paris, 1944).

---

* Since this series is intended for English readers only, many references in the original articles of the DS to publications in foreign languages have been omitted. All titles of primary sources have been translated into their English equivalents. When quotations from secondary sources are given in the body of the text, reference is made in the footnotes to the book or article from which the translation has been made.

⁷ See G. Fessard, *De l'actualité historique*, vol. 1, 173ff.

⁸ Saint Catherine of Siena, *Prayers* 24; quoted by Paul VI in his homily of December, 1965, *Acta Apostolicae Sedis* 58 (1966) 58.

NOTES TO CHAPTER 4

¹ Plato, *Republic* 9.589a.

² See E. des Places, *Lexique de Platon*, Les belles lettres, vol. 1 (Paris, 1964) 183-184.

³ Plotinus, *Enneads* 1.1.10 and 5.1.10.

⁴ E.-B. Allo, *Seconde épître aux Corinthiens*, Études bibliques (Paris, 1937) 137.

NOTES TO CHAPTER 5

¹ Origen, *The Song of Songs, Commentary and Homilies*, ACW 26, 24-30.

² Origen, *Homilies on Numbers* 24.2.

³ Origen, *Discussion with Heraclides* 11 and 16-23.

⁴ Ibid., 16.

⁵ O. Rousseau in his introduction to *Homélies sur le Cantique*, SC 27bis, 21.

⁶ Origen, *Homilies on Leviticus* 14.3.

⁷ Origen, *Homilies on Romans* 7.4.

⁸ Origen, *Homilies on Genesis* 13.4. Some other passages of Origen where the term "interior man" is used are: Ibid., 1.13 and 15; *Homilies on Exodus* 2.2; 8.6; 9.4; 10.3; *Homilies on Leviticus* 1.1 and 3.7; *Homilies on Jeremiah* 1.13; *Commentary on Romans* 1.19 and 2.13; *On First Principles* 4.3.7 and 4.9; *Against Celsus* 2.48; 6.63; 7.38; 7.46.

⁹ See *Orientalia christiana analecta*, vol. 117 (Rome, 1938) 5-8.

¹⁰ Gregory of Nyssa († after 394) also uses the term "interior man." For example: *On Virginity* 23.7; see 20.1; *Letters* 2.17; *On the Song of Songs* 1 and 14.

¹¹ Cassian, *Conferences*, preface see *Institutes* 2.9.1 and 3.

¹² J. Leroy, "Le cénobitisme chez Cassien," *RAM* 43 (1967) 155, n. 95.

¹³ Cassian, *Conferences* 7.2.1; see *Institutes* 5.11.11.

¹⁴ Cassian, *Conferences* 16.22.2. Other uses of "interior man" in Cassian are: *Institutes* 2.14; 5.13 and 21; 12.11.3 and 29.2; *Conferences* 3.7 and 8; 4.19; 5.9; 6.10.1; 7.2.3; 7.3.1; 7.5.6; 7.81; 7.15; 7.16; 7.21; 8.3; 9.21; 22.3; 22.6; 22.14; 22.15; 23.1; 23.11; 24.3.4. On Cassian, see DS, vol. 2, cols. 214-276, esp. cols. 220 and 225.

¹⁵ Plotinus, *Enneads* 5.1.10; 5.1.6-10.

[16] Porphyry, *Aids to the Study of the Intelligibles*, chaps. 37 and 43-45, in the edition of B. Mommert (Leipzig, 1907) 33-34, 36-38.

[17] Augustine, *On Order* 1.1.2-3.

[18] Augustine, *Confessions* 7.21.27.

[19] Augustine, *Magnitude of the Soul*, 28.55.

[20] Augustine, *On Genesis against the Manicheans* 1.27.28; see also *Unfinished Work on Genesis* 16.60; *Literal Commentary on Genesis* 3.20.30-32.

[21] Augustine, *The Teacher* 1.2.

[22] Augustine, *On True Religion* 30.72: "Do not go out of yourself; return to yourself; truth dwells in the inner man."

[23] This is a very ancient theme going back to Anaxagoras which has found its way into the *Hortensius* of Cicero through the *Proteptica* of Aristotle.

[24] Augustine, *83 Questions* 51.4: "...without any creature being placed between them."

[25] Augustine, *On the Trinity* 1.1ff; *Letters* 147, written around 413 to Paulina, 1.2; *On the Soul and Its Origin* 4.14.20.

[26] See, for example, Augustine, *Letters* 147.17.41 to 20.48.

[27] See Augustine *Confessions* 10.6-8; *Homilies on the Gospel of John* 8.9; *Sermons* 28.2. Along this line, Augustine speaks of the eye of the heart (*On Psalm 26* in *Sermons* 2.15), or the eye of the spirit (*On the Grace of Christ* 15.16), of the blindness of the heart (*Homilies on the Gospel of John* 1.19), of the mouth of the heart (*On Psalm 125*.5), of the ear of the heart (*Homilies on the Gospel of John* 1.19; *On Psalm 147*.5), of the tongue of the heart (ibid. 8), of the song of the heart (*On Psalm 86*.1), of "a spiritual contact with a pure heart," which Christ awaits from Mary Magdalen (*Homilies on the First Epistle of John* 3.1).

NOTES TO CHAPTER 6

[1] See DS, vol. 6, cols. 1241-1265.

[2] Sometimes the expression used is *homo carnalis*.

[3] William of Saint-Thierry, *On the Nature and Dignity of Love* 9.

[4] William of Saint-Thierry, *The Enigma of Faith* 6.

[5] Ibid., 84.

[6] William of Saint-Thierry, *The Mirror of Faith* PL 180, 390d.; in his commentary *On the Song of Songs* 1, he speaks equivalently of "a sense of life."

[7] William of Saint-Thierry, *The Enigma of Faith* 20 and 84.

[8] William of Saint-Thierry, *On the Nature and Dignity of Love* 14.

[9] Ibid., 23, 38, and 43.

[10] On the subject of the influence of Origen on William, see DS, vol. 6, col. 1253; also the introduction of J.-M. Déchanet in his edition of *Exposé sur le Cantique*, SC 82, 30-42; J. Walsh, "Guillaume...et les sens spirituels," RAM 35 (1959) 37-42. On the three major steps of spiritual progress according to William, see DS, vol. 6, cols. 1256-1259 (e.g. *On the Nature and Dignity of Love* 15-20).

[11] The expression appears when he quotes 2 Cor. 4:16 (*On Grace and Free Will* 4, 12, 14, 49; *Letters* 254); in other places he gives it the meaning of conscience (*On the Song of Songs* 82.6), as distinguished from the spiritual man (ibid., 24.6); the interior man is said to be adorned with *fides* and *intellectus* (ibid., 16.2). Finally, Bernard puts it in opposition to the exterior man without further explanation in *Sermons on Various Subjects* 32.1.

[12] Richard of Saint-Victor, *Questions on the Epistle to the Romans* 158; see *Questions on 2 Corinthians* 12.

[13] Richard of Saint-Victor, *Note on Psalm 80*.

[14] Richard of Saint-Victor, *On the Learning of the Interior Man* 2.8; *Benjamin major* 5; Hugh of Saint-Victor, *On Noah's Ark* 4.8.

[15] Richard of Saint-Victor, *On the Learning of the Interior Man* 1.19; see *Note on Psalm 80*.

[16] Richard of Saint-Victor, *Explanation of the Song of Songs* 15.

[17] Richard of Saint-Victor, *Note on Psalm 118*.

[18] Richard of Saint-Victor, *Benjamin minor* 70; see *Benjamin major* 2.17.

[19] Richard of Saint-Victor, *Benjamin major* 2.7, *passim*.

[20] Hugh of Saint-Victor, *Homilies on Ecclesiastes* 12; see *On the Sacraments* 1.6; Richard of Saint-Victor, *Explanation of the Song of Songs*, prologue.

[21] Richard of Saint-Victor, *On the State of the Interior Man* 1.1; see 34.

[22] Richard of Saint-Victor, *On the Apocalypse* 1.1.

[23] Richard of Saint-Victor, *Benjamin major* 2.19; see 13.16 and 17.

[24] Richard of Saint-Victor, *Benjamin major* 2.17; see *Note on Psalm 40*.

[25] Richard of Saint-Victor, *On the Extermination of Evil* 3.18.

[26] Thomas Aquinas, *Summa theologica* I, q. 75, a. 4, ad 1.

[27] See, for example, Thomas Aquinas, *On the Epistle to the Ephesians*, chap. 3, fourth lecture; sometimes he defines the expression by *ratio* and *mens*: *On the Epistle to the Romans*, chap. 7, fourth lecture; see *On the Second Epistle to the Corinthians*, chap. 4, fifth lecture.

[28] Thomas Aquinas, *On the First Epistle to the Corinthians*,

chap. 2, third lecture; see *On the Epistle to the Romans*, chap. 7, third lecture. In II^a^II^ae^, q. 25, a. 7, c., by making use of the notion of the interior man, Thomas specifies how the good man is to love himself.

[29] Bonaventure, *Commentary on the Sentences*, II, dist. 24, pars 2, dubium 3.

[30] Bonaventure, *Breviloquium*, part 2, chap. 11.

[31] See DS, vol. 3, cols. 42-44; see vol. 2, cols. 592-593 and 1970.

[32] Once he has presented the general data, David then uses a more definite vocabulary for the three powers of memory, intellect, and will, in order to explain, for example, the struggle against the capital sins. In his third book, "On Seven Means of Spiritual Progress," which is the richest because he there handles the most spiritual subjects, he no longer uses the term "interior man."

[33] Ms., see DS, vol. 7, col. 191.

[34] Ms., see ibid., col. 302.

[35] See DS, vol. 5, cols. 650-661.

[36] The meaning of the expression "interior man" as used by Eckhart has been treated in the article "Divinisation," DS, vol. 4, cols. 1432-1439, esp. 1436.

[37] See *The Book of Divine Comfort* in *Meister Eckhart, A Modern Translation* (New York, 1941) 59-60.

[38] Augustine, *On True Religion* 39.72.

[39] Denis the Areopagite, *On the Divine Names* 1.6.

[40] V. Lossky, *Théologie negative et connaissance de Dieu chez Maître Eckhart* (Paris, 1960) 30.

[41] *The Aristocrat* in *Meister Eckhart, A Modern Translation* (New York, 1941) 74.

[42] See, above all, the work of V. Lossky cited in note 40. The article "Eckhart," DS, vol. 4, cols. 93-116, offers a general account; see also DS, vol. 3, cols. 1436-1437.

[43] John Tauler, *Sermons* 15: "Glorify me, Father, with the glory...." The numbering used here follows that of the French translation *Sermons de Tauler*, by E. Hugueney, G. Théry, and A. L. Corin, 3 vols. (Paris 1927-1935).

[44] See DS, vol. 3, cols. 1440-1442. As for Henry Suso, see, e.g., *The Life of the Servant*, 2nd pt., chap. 49, and the 9th letter in *The Little Book of Letters*. See also art. "Henri Suso," DS, vol. 7, esp. cols. 246-255.

[45] Henry Suso, *The Life of the Servant*, 2nd pt., chap. 2. For the principal passages of Ruysbroeck on the "interior man," we refer to the following works of the Ruusbroec-Genootschap, *Jan von Ruusbroec Werken*, vols. 1 and 3 (Tielt, 1944 and 1947): *Die geestelike Brulocht (The Spiritual Espousals)*, book 2, vol. 1,

143-238; *Van den blickenden Steen* (*The Book of the Sparkling Stone*), vol. 3, 5-6, 14-22; *Van den seven Sloten* (*The Seven Euclosures*), vol. 1, 175-183; *Een Spieghel der eeuwigher Saligheit* (*The Mirror of Eternal Blessedness*), vol. 3, 198-217; *Van seven Trappen* (*The Seven Steps of the Laddar of Spiritual Love*), vol. 3, 235-263.

46 *The Imitation of Christ* 3.54 *in fine.*

47 See DS, vol. 1, cols. 1730-1738.

48 See DS, vol. 1, cols. 458-459.

NOTES TO CHAPTER 7

1 For example, authors will speak, with Benoit de Canfield (†1610), of the interior operation of God (*Reigle de perfection* [Douai, 1632] 21), of the interior will of God (45, 54, 198), of the "interior or contemplative life" (199, 276-277); with Cardinal Bérulle († 1629), of interior occupations (*Letter 154*, in *Oeuvres* [Paris, 1856], col. 1492), of the interior and exterior way (*Opuscule de piété* 125, ibid., col. 1157) with Constantin de Barbanson (†1631), of tranquility, of exercise, of interior stages (*Les secrets sentiers de l'amour divin* [Cologne, 1623]). Jean-Jacques Olier († 1657) begins his *Introduction à la vie et aux vertus chrétiennes*, chs. 2 and 3 (Paris, 1657), by distinguishing the exterior mysteries and the interior mysteries of Christ. As early as 1608, the famous Jesuit Pierre Coton († 1626) published the *Intérieure occupation d'une âme dévote* (see DS, vol. 2, col. 2425). Bernadin de Paris (†1685) calls two of his works *Le religieux intérieur* (Paris, 1663) and *L'intérieur de Jésus Christ en l'eucharistie* (Paris 1671), while Louis François d'Argentan published the works of Jean de Bernières-Louvigny under the title *Le chrétien intérieur ou la conformité intérieure*... (Paris, 1661). A list of spiritual books that use this term would be very lengthy.

2 Martin Niger (Lenoir), a hermit of Saint Augustine, *Le tableau raccourci de l'home intérieur* (Rouen, 1605); Cornélius Jansenius, bishop of Ypres, *Oratio de interioris hominis reformatione habita in monasterio Affligemensi* (Antwerp, 1624; FT: Paris, 1644); Vincent of Rouen, a tertiary regular of Saint Francis, *Exercices de l'homme intérieur* (Paris, 1650); Pierre-Thomas de Sainte-Marie, a discalced Carmelite, *Les délices de l'homme intérieur, ou le Cantique des cantiques exposé*... (Rouen, 1653); Cyprien de la Nativité de la Vierge, a discalced Carmelite, *Exercices de l'homme intérieur*, that we have not been able to consult (Paris, 1660; see DS, vol. 2, col. 2671); Timothée Brianson de Raynier, a Minim, *L'homme intérieur ou l'idée du parfait chrétien* (Aix, 1662); A. Nicholas Robine, Augustinian, *Exercices de l'homme intérieur dans la pratique de l'oraison mentale*, 2 vols. of medita-

tions (Paris, 1691); Domenico Ricci, Dominican, *Homo interior juxta doctoris angelici doctrinam...ad explodendos errores Michaelis Molinos*, 3 vols. (Naples, 1709); later, Ch. Le Gac, *Manual de l'homme intérieur* (San-Brieuc and Paris, 1819).

[3] James Alvarez de Paz, *De exterminatione et promotione boni* (Lyons, 1613), book 2, 2nd and 3rd sections: "*De mortfiicatione hominis exterioris...interioris.*"

[4] Jean-Pierre Camus, *Traité de la reformation intérieur* and *De la sindérèse* (Paris, 1631).

[5] Maximilien Sandeus, *Pro theologica mystica clavis* (Cologne, 1640) 228-232; see also 208, 254-257.

[6] Antoine Civoré, *Les secrets de la science des saints* (Lille, 1651) 259-303: definitions of mystical terms.

[7] Honoré de Sainte-Marie, *Tradition des Pères...sur la contemplation*, vol. 1 (Paris, 1708), 2nd part, 247-341: "Des termes de la Théologie mystique," where our expression does not occur.

[8] See DS, vol. 5, cols. 1643-1644.

[9] Maximien de Bernezay, *Traité de la vie intérieure*, 3rd ed. (Orléans, 1686), preface; permission to publish given in 1685.

[10] Ibid., 1-2; see 129. Henri-Marie Boudon († 1702) offers the same synthetic concept of the interior man in *L'homme intérieur ou Vie du V. P. Jean Chrysostome* (Paris, 1684), chap. 1: "De l'homme intérieur."

[11] Alippe de la Vierge Marie, *L'homme intérieur selon l'esprit du Bx Francois de Sales* (Lyon, 1657).

[12] Ibid., 4-5.

[13] Jean Aumont, *L'ouverture intérieure du Royaume de l'Agneau occis dans nos coeurs* (Paris, 1660).

[14] Ibid., 156-158.

[15] Ibid., 122-129, 366-368, *passim;* see also the first illustration in the work.

[16] Ibid., 12.

[17] Ibid., 576.

[18] Ibid., 96, 198.

[19] Ibid., 390.

[20] Ibid., 479.

[21] Ibid., 329.

[22] Ibid., 486.

[23] Jean-Joseph Surin, *Catéchisme spirituel* (Paris, 1657), 5th part, chap. 5.

[24] Jean-Joseph Surin, *Guide spirituel*, ed. M. de Certeau, Christus 12 (Paris, 1963), 2nd part, chap. 8, 129-134; this text is used in certain editions of the *Catéchisme spirituel*, e.g., that of Paris, 1683, vol. 2, 8th part, chap. 8.

[25] See, for example, Jean-Joseph Surin, *Les fondements de la vie spirituelle* (Paris, 1667), bk. 1, chap. 1; bk. 4, chap. 2 and chap. 4.

[26] Louis Lallement, *Doctrine spirituelle*, Fifth Principle, chap. 2, art. 2.

[27] Jean Rigoleuc, *Le pur amour*, chap. 1: "De la garde du coeur"; in P. Champion, *La vie du P. J. Rigoleuc...avec ses traités* (Paris, 1686; re-edited A. Hamon, Paris, 1931).

[28] Francois Guilloré, *Conférences spirituelles*, 2nd ed. (Paris, 1689), vol. 2, bk. 2, conf. 3, 223-254.

[29] A. Lalande, *Vocabulaire technique et critique de la philosophie*, 7th ed. (Paris, 1956), 329-330.

[30] Ibid.

BIBLIOGRAPHY

Chapter 1

Eliade, M., *Myths, Dreams and Mysteries*. New York: 1961.
———, *Rites and Symbols of Initiation. The Mystery of Birth and Rebirth*. New York: 1965.
Hultkranz, A., *Conceptions of the Soul among the North American Indians*. Stockholm: 1953.
Onians, R.B., *The Origins of European Thought about the Body, the Mind, the Soul, the World, Time and Fate*. 2nd ed. Cambridge: 1954.
Studies in the Cosmological Ideas and Social Values of African Peoples, presented by Daryll Forde. London: 1954. Reprinted 1965.

Chapter 2

Beauchamp, E., *The Bible and the Universe*. Westminster, Md.: 1963.
Cerfaux, L., *Christ in the Theology of St. Paul*. New York: 1959.
De Fraine, J., *Adam and the Family of Man*. New York: 1965.
———, *The Bible and the Origin of Man*. 2nd ed. New York: 1967.
la Potterie, I. de, and Lyonnet, S., *The Christian Lives by the Spirit*. Staten Island, New York: 1971.
Léon-Dufour, X., *Dictionary of Biblical Theology*. London-Dublin: 1967.
Prat, F., *The Theology of St. Paul*. 2 vols. Westminster, Md.: 1952.
Schnackenburg, R., *The Moral Teaching of the New Testament*. Freiburg: 1965.

Chapter 4

Plato, *The Republic*. The Penguin Classics, L 48. Middlesex: 1959.

Plotinus, *The Enneads*. 3rd ed. New York: 1962.

Chapter 5

Augustine, *Confessions*. FC 21.

————, *Letters 131-164*. FC 20.

————, *Magnitude of the Soul*. FC 4.

————, *On the Psalms*. ACW 29 and 30.

————, *The Teacher*. FC 59.

————, *The Trinity*. FC 45.

————, *Homilies on the Gospel of John; Homilies on the First Epistle of John*. NPNF, 1st ser., vol. 7.

Cassian, John, *Conferences; Institutes*. NPNF, 2nd ser., vol. 11.

Gregory of Nyssa, *On Virginity; Letters*. NPNF, 2nd ser., vol. 5.

Origen, *Contra Celsum*. Cambridge: 1953.

————, *The Song of Songs, Commentary and Homilies*. ACW 26.

Plotinus, *The Enneads*. 3rd ed. New York: 1962.

Chapter 6

Bernard, *Letters*.

Bernard, *Letters*. Chicago: 1953.

————, *On the Song of Songs* I. CF 4.

————, *Sermons on the Canticle of Canticles*. Dublin: 1920.

————, *Works*. London: 1889.

Bonaventure, *Breviloquium*. St. Louis: 1946.

————, *The Works of Bonaventure*. Paterson: 1960.

The Exemplar: Life and Writings of Bl. Henry Suso, O.P. Dubuque: 1962.

Imitation of Christ. New York: 1958.

Meister Eckhart, A Modern Translation. New York: 1941.

Pseudo-Dionysius, *Works*. London: 1897.

Richard of Saint-Victor, *Selected Writings on Contemplation*. New York: 1957.

Ruysbroeck, Jan van, *The Spiritual Espousals*. New York: 1953.

Signpost to Perfection. A Selection from the Sermons of Johann Tauler. St. Louis and London: 1958.

Thomas Acquinas, *Summa theologica*. 2nd ed. New York: 1912-1936.

William of Saint-Thierry, *The Mirror of Faith*. Fleur de lys series 15. London: 1959.

————, *On the Nature and Dignity of Love*. Fleur de lys series 10. London: 1956.